WHAT ABOUT Unanswered Prayer?

To our son Matthew Douglas Rumford,
who told me after my first sermon on this topic,
"Dad, that should be your next book!"

WHAT ABOUT
Unanswered Prayer?

Douglas J. Rumford

TYNDALE HOUSE PUBLISHERS, INC. | WHEATON, ILLINOIS

Visit Tyndale's exciting Web site at www.tyndale.com

Published in association with the literary agency of Alive Communications, Inc., 7680 Goddard Street, Suite 200, Colorado Springs, CO 80920.

Designed by Justin Ahrens

People's names and certain details of the stories in this book have been changed to protect the privacy of the individuals involved. However, the facts of what happened and the underlying principles have been conveyed as accurately as possible.

Material in chapter 4 on wearing the armor of God is drawn from notes the author originally wrote for the *Spiritual Renewal Bible,* copyright © 1998, Tyndale House Publishers, Inc.

Library of Congress Cataloging-in-Publication Data

Rumford, Douglas J.
   What about unanswered prayer? / Douglas J. Rumford.
      p. cm.
   Includes bibliographical references.
   ISBN 0-8423-7403-5 (pbk.)
   1. Prayer—Christianity.   I. Title.
BV220.R7942000
248.3′2—dc21   99-086461

Printed in the United States of America

06   05   04   03   02   01
7   6   5   4   3   2

CONTENTS

INTRODUCTION

The "Whys" of Unanswered Prayer

Prayer is a human instinct. We all cry out for help beyond ourself. In desperate situations, in deep distress, in times of ache and longing, we call out to God: *God, if you're really there, now is when I need you. God, if you really love me, now is the time to come through.* The stakes are often very high:

A dear family friend calls to tell you that she's losing her job, her ex-husband is six months behind in child support payments, and her car just broke down.

Your child doesn't want to have anything to do with the values you've tried to instill in him since birth, and you're scared.

You can't seem to cope like you used to, and the pressures are getting overwhelming.

You have worked and worked and worked to establish yourself in your profession, but someone is unfairly questioning your integrity and spreading rumors

about you. You're starting to see everything you've
worked for crumble.

You're alone, so very, very alone.

So you pray. To the best of your abilities, you really
pray. So much is riding on that prayer. That's why it
hurts so much when no answer comes.

A PAINFUL QUESTION

Why do some prayers seem to go unanswered? This
question has too much pain behind it to answer with
glib, pious platitudes. I think, for example, of a man I
know whose marriage ended, despite his desperate ef-
forts to save it. Pouring out his anguish to me one day,
he answered my unspoken question: "I prayed and
prayed and prayed." Looking him in the eye, I knew that
quoting a Bible passage like "All things work together
for good" and then saying a quick prayer would only
wound his soul even more. It would discount his suffering and the genuine mystery of life in this fallen world.

I began reflecting on unanswered prayer in the tenth
grade when a friend was seriously injured in a car acci-
dent. My friends and I prayed and prayed for him, but
he died. I didn't get it. Even at that age I wanted to believe God would help us but felt myself giving in to a
kind of fatalism, a resignation that "whatever will be will
be." A few months later a friend gave me a book called
Essays on Prayer (InterVarsity Press, 1968). As I read
through the table of contents, I saw the chapter titled

"Some Pray and Die" and immediately turned to it and began reading. The essay was written by an anonymous army chaplain serving in Africa during World War II. He began with these words: "I wish that people would stop writing about people who pray on rafts and get rescued. Because they don't all get rescued. What about the fellows who pray regularly and get killed regularly? What was wrong with their prayers?"

The chaplain went on to tell the story of a devout young Christian who arrived in Africa on assignment as a pilot. Within the first day, the pilot had sought out the chaplain and attended chapel services. The next day he prayed with the chaplain and boarded his plane to fly his mission. But he never returned. The chaplain wrote, "'What was wrong with my prayers?' I asked myself as I stood by the fearful wreckage of the plane he tried so bravely to bring in safely. Other people's prayers are answered. What's wrong with ours? Who gets the breaks in prayer?"

THE COST OF LETTING UNANSWERED PRAYER STOP OUR PRAYING

This author's raw, blunt emotion pierced my heart. Here was someone, a spiritual leader no less, who was honest enough to admit his disappointment, confusion, and heartache about tragically unanswered prayer. His candor gave me hope. It was not the hope that comes from getting all the answers. It was the hope that comes from seeing courage and conviction despite great pain, deep disappointment, and threatening obstacles.

If we are going to grow spiritually, we must learn what

to do about unanswered prayer. In fact, for some, resolving this issue is critical to developing a positive relationship with God.

Perhaps there is no more common spiritual struggle than the one that results when we don't get what we prayed for. In *Letters to Malcolm*, C. S. Lewis said, "Every war, every famine or plague, and almost every deathbed is a monument to a petition that was not granted." Then how do we respond? Failure to understand is one of the greatest obstacles to becoming all we long to be. Unanswered prayer can block deepening fellowship with God, even as a refusal of help from a friend can hurt the friendship. It can smother joy, defeat hope, and erode faith.

I have been trying to make prayer a way of life. I want prayer to be my first response, not my last resort. But in order for that to happen, I need to face the fact of unanswered prayer. Why doesn't God come through sometimes—especially in some very important times? If that's not *your* question, it's one that your friends and neighbors are asking. I have listened when people asked:

Why didn't God answer my prayers when my child was sick? Instead, he died.

Why didn't God hear my prayers for my marriage? Instead, my spouse had an affair.

Why didn't God answer my prayer for my career? Instead, I lost my job.

Why didn't God hear our prayers for our unborn child? Instead, she has birth defects.

Why? Why? Why?

When we ask tough questions, we've got to get ready for tough answers. When we ask heart questions, we've got to dig a little deeper to understand the purposes of God.

EVEN IF WE KNEW . . .

It's important to acknowledge up front that we cannot know all the reasons for unanswered prayer. Sometimes, the reasons for God's apparent silence are a mystery. (We will look at the issue of mystery in one of the upcoming chapters.) In many cases, however, even if we did know the reason for a particular unanswered prayer, the knowledge would not comfort us. Ultimately, comfort comes only from the Lord.

Understanding unanswered prayer is not so much about gaining information as it is about understanding who we are spiritually and what we believe about God. Wrestling with unanswered prayer may cause our faith to grow in ways it never would grow otherwise. It can drive us to search our heart, examine our faith, and consider deeply our relationship with God.

While we can't always know the reasons for unanswered prayer in specific instances, the Bible does give some clues as to why God may appear to be silent in response to the petitions of his people. In this book, I'm going to survey six reasons the Bible gives for unanswered prayer. This survey is suggestive, not exhaustive. Please note that I'm presenting these principles in the order in which they appear in the Bible, not in any order of priority. After considering each reason, we will look at how to live with unanswered prayers.

One note about the term *unanswered prayer:* The reality is that no prayer goes unanswered. The Lord either says *yes* or *no* or *wait.* This book addresses those situations when God seems to be saying *no* or *wait.* My hope is that you and I may come to the point where we can see *wait*— or even *no*—as the Lord's *yes* to our heart's deepest desires and needs.

I believe there are some reading this book who haven't prayed in years because of a prayer God never seemed to answer. If this is your situation, I'm hopeful that as you read, your heart, mind, and spirit will be touched. In fact, I hope that by the end of the book, you will be ready to get on your knees again—not because you've been given easy answers—but because you've found encouraging truth and practical principles that can soothe the ache, stimulate renewed vision, and guide you as you continue to pray.

CHAPTER ONE

The Principle of Progressive Victory

Sometimes unanswered prayer is simply the first step on the way to a wonderful answer that needs to come in stages. We see this principle when God's people began to conquer the Promised Land. The people of Israel had been in Egypt for over four hundred years. They had done well in Egypt in the time of Joseph but later experienced oppression and persecution. They were subjected to slavery for the great building projects of the pharaohs. They left Egypt as a rather ragtag group, moving through the wilderness into Canaan, the land God had promised as their new homeland. But they faced tremendous opposition. Though God gave them victories like the one at Jericho, he didn't answer all their prayers right away. They didn't conquer the Promised Land instantly. The Lord's strategy is described in Deuteronomy 7:21-24:

> "No, do not be afraid of those nations, for the
> Lord your God is among you, and he is a great and

awesome God. The Lord your God will drive those nations out ahead of you little by little. You will not clear them away all at once, for if you did, the wild animals would multiply too quickly for you. But the Lord your God will hand them over to you. He will throw them into complete confusion until they are destroyed. He will put their kings in your power, and you will erase their names from the face of the earth. No one will be able to stand against you, and you will destroy them all.

This is a fascinating passage. The Lord promises to drive out the nations before Israel little by little, instead of all at once. And we ask, *Why little by little? Why not all at once, God? Wouldn't it be easier just to get it all over with, once and for all? Wouldn't it be more efficient? Wouldn't it be a dramatic display of God's power of the ungodly? Wouldn't it be a great way to encourage the Israelites? What could possibly be wrong with driving the nations out quickly, giving Israel a complete victory immediately?*

Listen to the reason: "for . . . the wild animals will multiply too quickly for you." In other words, answering their prayer for complete victory immediately could bring them ultimate defeat! The simple fact is that the ecological balance of the food chain would be so disrupted by a radical depopulation that it would threaten the fledgling nation. God was giving the Israelites protection by answering their prayers little by little.

The first reason for unanswered prayer is the principle of progressive victory. God may say no to help us move forward in safety. God may say no because an immediate yes would hurt us far more than we might realize.

WHO KNOWS BEST?

When bringing our requests to God, we often can't resist advising him on how to answer them. In fact, many of us are discouraged if we can't give God a few ideas. But we need to remember that our thoughts are not God's thoughts. God is not limited to the possibilities we see. He sees consequences we cannot anticipate.

K. P. Yohannan, founder of the evangelistic mission society Gospel for Asia, tells of God's delay in answering his prayers for funding his new mission organization:

> I never told anyone that I eventually would need such huge sums of money. They already thought I was crazy for wanting to support eight or ten missionaries a month out of my own income. What would they think if I said I needed millions of dollars a year to field an army of God? But I knew it was possible. Several Western missionary societies and charities already were dealing with annual budgets that size. I saw no reason why we couldn't do the same. But as logical as it all was in my mind, I had some bitter lessons to learn.[1]

K. P. was not able to get funding immediately. But as he prayed and shared his vision, he clarified his thinking about the mission and the best way to involve people. Then one day, a friend suggested he develop a "Dollar-a-Day" pledge program to support native missionaries. That program has become the backbone of the mission's financial strategy. He writes, "During those days our needs continued to be met on a day-to-day basis, and I never had to borrow from the missionary support funds. I am convinced now that God knew the many trials ahead and wanted to teach us to have and trust in Him alone—even when I couldn't see Him."[2]

K. P. thought he knew the right answer to his prayers: God should provide immediate funding for his new mission. But God knew best about what kind of answer K. P. needed and when he needed it.

When I was pastor of First Presbyterian Church in Fresno, California, we once wrestled with what to do with a house that was on property we had purchased to be our new parking lot. The church was located in the downtown area. When I first arrived, we had hundreds driving in to attend worship, but our parking lot held only seventy-five cars. So we used adjacent vacant lots. But the properties didn't belong to us. If they were sold, our future would be radically affected. So we bought the rest of the city block across the street. We demolished an abandoned car dealership and two houses that were beyond repair. But there was a fourplex apartment with six thousand square feet that could either be relocated or used for some purpose. For over a year we prayed earnestly and discussed countless possibilities for what we could do with this building. Nothing was working out. Days before we were going to level it, a member of our congregation had the brainstorm: *Let's make it a leadership house for urban ministry.* In an amazingly short time we had a full-fledged partnership with a parachurch organization to support urban ministry leaders. The "Pink House," as we called it (based on its color, of course!), became a means of transforming lives and the community, as Christians with a heart for the city moved in—and then often moved out to buy a home in the neighborhood.

Looking back, we saw that the resources for the Pink House were not in place during the months we had begun praying. We had to go through various stages: acquire the property, demolish the other houses, pray, and clarify our vision. Then God brought a person to us who could pull it all together. In God's time, everything came together. Amazing!

God can do more in a moment than we can do in a lifetime. When we fret, we lose sight of both God's purposes and God's power. He is literally orchestrating a work far greater than any of us can imagine. For a while, we only hear our little part. We may find it very difficult to have so few notes and so many rests. But then we hear God's symphony, and we understand.

WHAT SORTS OF BEASTS THREATEN US?

God protected the Israelites by answering their prayers in stages so they wouldn't be devoured by too much success. Are there ways this principle applies to us? I would like to suggest at least four situations in which God may answer our prayers progressively in order to protect us. Let me compare these to the beasts that needed to be kept under control in the Promised Land.

THE BEAST OF OVEREXTENSION
In a day of both endless need and boundless opportunities, many of us are tempted to get overextended using

our spiritual gifts and resources. I can tell story after story about myself and others who have taken off like a rocket, only to burn out in exhaustion. But I also know stories of people who were protected from burnout because their prayers were seemingly unanswered.

I have a friend, for example, who prayed for his new consulting business to succeed. He had a very ambitious plan and enthusiasm to match. Still, he had far fewer clients than he wanted. He added staff much more slowly than he had anticipated. Finally, about seven years into the venture, momentum picked up. "You know, Doug," he said, "I shudder now to think what would have happened if we had met my initial growth projections. I had to go slow in order to go fast."

As another friend who preaches the "build slowly, build solidly" principle points out, lasting works require strong foundations. Firm foundations must come first—and they take time to build.

Is the beast of overextension threatening you? Think about the implications of your prayers: if God answered yes, how would it impact your time, energy, resources, priorities, and relationships? Could it be that God wants you to build a stronger base so you can reach your full potential?

THE BEAST OF PRIDE

Answered prayer can be twisted into a means of pride. A blessing may exceed our ability to live humbly. We all know stories of those who achieved too much too soon, whose success destroyed them.

The Corinthians were victims of pride. As God

blessed them, they began to boast in their special relationship with him. They thought of themselves as above God's law. Their fellowship degenerated into cliques. They misused their spiritual gifts—and in general made a mess of things.

We may pray to succeed, but we may not be ready to handle success. God may say no as a sign of protection. The whole principle here is the law of unintended consequences. We may not understand the consequences of what we pray for. So God may give us progressive victory. Are we able to remember that God gives the growth (see 1 Corinthians 3:6)? We need to guard our heart against the invasion of pride that can sneak in with some answered prayers.

THE BEAST OF LIMITED VISION

Shortly after graduating from seminary, I asked one of my favorite professors, Dr. Richard Lovelace, author of *Dynamics of Spiritual Life,* to speak at a pastors' conference. He readily agreed. Several months later, I called and asked if he would speak for another event. This time he paused. "Doug," he responded, "I feel strongly that I should say no. I don't want to disappoint you, but I'm learning that I must say no more often in order to make room for others to serve." Dr. Lovelace wasn't God's answer to my prayers. I was initially disappointed. But in reflecting on what he said, I realized that God may say no so that we will look in other directions, involve other people, or think things through again.

When we are praying, we often fasten on one solution for our problem, or one person we want to involve in a project, or one location for a particular event. Our preoccupation may blind us to the creative solutions God has. He may want us to involve underutilized people or experiment with an idea or a place that others haven't considered. God is very creative—he wants us to break the grip of the beasts of the ordinary, the predictable, and the status quo.

THE BEAST OF INDIVIDUALISM

Success can cut us off from community. It can insulate us from others when we most need to be connected to them. God has designed us to be interconnected and interdependent. Imagine a commercial gardener who prays for a bumper crop to bring a nice profit. He may even desire to give a portion of that profit to God's work. But thrusting a very large quantity of that particular product into the market all at one time might create a glut and result in a serious loss to other growers. A surplus of that commodity might lessen the demand for another item, creating hardships for someone else. The bountiful crop could affect import and export quotations, the balance of trade operations, and many other aspects of the economy. Our finite minds cannot encompass all the ramifications of a single situation. But we need to learn to trust that God considers the impact of a situation on all parties involved. [3]

IS THIS WHY MY PRAYER IS STILL UNANSWERED?

Consider your past prayers. Are there times you have seen this principle of progressive victory in operation?

Have you ever seen your prayers answered in stages? I have a friend who desperately wanted to be a college professor. She prepared faithfully, but God closed the doors. So she pursued other areas to exercise her gifts and started her family. Now God is opening the doors for her to teach at the college level. "God's timing is amazing," she said to me recently. "I really wasn't ready when I thought I was. Over these last few years I've had the chance to learn so much more about working with people—things that will add so much to the classroom. And I have a family I might have passed up if I'd gone into full-time academia. I can't imagine missing that!"

What about your present prayers? Is there an area in which you may be getting too far ahead without considering the beasts of unintended consequences? Take inventory of your prayers using this question: "If God answered this prayer in the way I'm hoping for, how would it affect me, my family, my work, my ministry, and my community?" Even if asking this question doesn't give you additional understanding, it may help you think more broadly.

HOW TO PRAY

As you and I pray, we must be aware that God may say no to protect us from the beasts of overextension, pride, limited vision, and individualism. At times, God is bringing progressive victory, for the beasts might slay us.

If you think you may be praying without sufficient regard to the beasts that might slay you, I suggest you ask

God for wisdom to see the present stage and for courage to endure over time—because receiving answers may take longer than you initially hoped. Pray for gratitude to appreciate the victory he is giving, as small as it may seem to be.

Above all, keep praying.

NOTES

1. K.P. Yohannan, *Revolution in World Mission* (Altamonte Springs, Fla.: Creation House, 1986), 77.

2. Ibid., 82.

3. Virginia Whiteman, *Mustard* (Wheaton, Ill.: Tyndale House Publishers, Inc., 1973), 90–91. Cited in Dick Eastman, *Change the World! School of Prayer* (Studio City, Calif.: World Literature Crusade, 1976), 119.

CHAPTER TWO

The Principle of Judgment

I was visiting a woman in the hospital who was not improving after chemotherapy for cancer. We had just read the Bible and prayed when Sherry looked up with tears in her eyes. "What have I done wrong?" she said. "I must have done something terrible to be suffering like this. . . ." Her voice trailed off in despair.

This kind of reaction is one I see often in response to illness—one I am eager to lovingly correct. Intentional sin had not caused Sherry's cancer. It was simply one of the mysteries of life. God was not judging her. She was experiencing the harsh reality of life in this fallen world.

Disappointment and suffering often lead people to search their hearts for causes of their pain. They assume that they must have done something wrong, something that is blocking their prayers. More often than not, they are experiencing false guilt.

Still, there are times when sin and judgment *are* directly behind unanswered prayer. We'll see this clearly later on as we look at the story of David and Bathsheba.

God judged their adultery and David's arranged killing of Bathsheba's husband, Uriah, by allowing their new-born child to die. The reality of God's judgment is hard to face, but it is one of the biblical reasons prayers may go unanswered.

Let me give a word of counsel and caution here: Please don't jump to the immediate conclusion that you are suffering the pain of unanswered prayer because God is judging your sin. Please don't. As I said earlier, I'm pre-senting possible reasons for unanswered prayer in the order they appear in the Bible, not in order of priority or probability. I need to address God's judgment because there are times when it does apply, but I hope you hear the pastoral heart in this counsel: Unless you are allowing intentional sin in your life, don't be quick to jump to the conclusion that you've been judged.

THE GUILT REACTION

Guilt is a powerful—and sometimes healthy—force in our life. It is often a fever of the soul warning us to re-pent, confess our sin, and be reconciled to the Lord and those we've offended.[1] But guilt can also be an in-appropriate reaction to suffering, including unan-swered prayer.

One kind of inappropriate reaction to suffering or unanswered prayer is false guilt. False guilt occurs when people like Sherry wrongly assume that God's apparent silence is clear evidence of sin.

Another inappropriate reaction is misplaced guilt—guilt feelings persuading us that difficulties in one area, such as unanswered prayer, are judgments for sin in some other area. A student who fails a test may think it's a judgment against her for fighting with her parents or gossiping about her classmates. An athlete who loses an important game may think God is judging him for impure thoughts and habits. A businessperson who loses a major customer may see the loss as judgment for sexual infidelity. Such conclusions are usually misguided, as we'll see later in this discussion.

A third inappropriate reaction is lack of guilt despite intentional sin. Some people feel no guilt even when they've committed a serious offense. This was the case with King David.

THE EXAMPLE OF DAVID

When his troops left for war, David stayed home and lost a far more significant battle: a battle for his heart. He saw Bathsheba, the wife of one of his soldiers, bathing and was consumed with lust for her. He slept with her, resulting in her pregnancy. Then began "Bathsheba-gate," a cover-up scheme that escalated to tragic proportions. First, David had Bathsheba's husband, Uriah, sent home on leave from the front lines. He was hoping Uriah would sleep with his wife and therefore appear to be responsible for the pregnancy. But Uriah followed a code of honor David hadn't counted on. When urged to sleep with his wife, Uriah refused. We read in 2 Samuel 11:9:

> But Uriah wouldn't go home. He stayed that night at the palace entrance with some of the king's

other servants. When David heard what Uriah had done, he summoned him and asked, "What's the matter with you? Why didn't you go home last night after being away for so long?" Uriah replied, "The Ark and the armies of Israel and Judah are living in tents, and Joab and his officers are camping in the open fields. How could I go home to wine and dine and sleep with my wife? I swear that I will never be guilty of acting like that."

Uriah couldn't indulge himself in pleasure while his comrades were on the battlefield. David certainly had had no such qualms! David tried to persuade Uriah a second time by getting him drunk. Still Uriah refused to go home. Finally, David took an unthinkable, desperate step. He sent Uriah back to the battlefront with his own death warrant. "So the next morning David wrote a letter to Joab and gave it to Uriah to deliver. The letter instructed Joab, 'Station Uriah on the front lines where the battle is fiercest. Then pull back so that he will be killed.' So Joab assigned Uriah to a spot close to the city wall where he knew the enemy's strongest men were fighting. And Uriah was killed along with several other Israelite soldiers" (2 Samuel 11:14-17).

When David learned of Uriah's death, he sloughed it off casually and, after her time of mourning, took Bathsheba as his wife. We see in David no evidence of an afflicted conscience, no expression of guilt, no awareness of the abomination of his actions. David's failure to acknowledge his guilt led God to take drastic steps to confront him.

SEEING THE TERRIBLE TRUTH

God sent the prophet Nathan to break through David's denial. Nathan told David a parable that slipped past his defenses like a stealth missile. In the story, a poor man who had only one lamb (not even a sheep!) was forced to give it up in order to feed the guest of a rich man who had many sheep. Indignant at the injustice, David pronounced immediate judgment on the rich man. Then, in words that sounded a fearful echo across the ages, Nathan thundered, "You are that man!"

Nathan's parable appealed to David's sense of honor and justice. It became a mirror in which he was forced to see himself. He broke immediately. Without denial, excuses, or blame, he confessed his sin:

> *Have mercy on me, O God,*
> *because of your unfailing love.*
> *Because of your great compassion,*
> *blot out the stain of my sins.*
> *Wash me clean from my guilt.*
> *Purify me from my sin.*
> *For I recognize my shameful deeds—*
> *they haunt me day and night.*
> *Against you, and you alone, have I sinned;*
> *I have done what is evil in your sight.*
> *You will be proved right in what you say,*
> *and your judgment against me is just.*
> *(Psalm 51:1-4)*

David saw the terrible truth of his offense and heard a terrible word of judgment: The child born of adultery would die.

PRAYING THROUGH

Faced with the truth, David began to pray. "After Nathan returned to his home, the Lord made Bathsheba's baby deathly ill. David begged God to spare the child. He went without food and lay all night on the bare ground. The leaders of the nation pleaded with him to get up and eat with them, but he refused" (2 Samuel 12:15-17).

David's insistent, intense prayer portrays a powerful expression of repentance, of seeking after God. David didn't turn away from God in his sin. He didn't resign himself as if he were dealing with a cold, unrelenting "fate."

Fate is the belief that there is a predetermined course of events beyond human control. In Greek mythology the Fates were the three goddesses who determined human life and destiny, apportioning a share of good and evil to each person at birth. The goddesses were often thought of as weavers and were portrayed in art and poetry as stern old women or as somber maidens. The decisions of the Fates could not be altered, even by the gods.

Fate and luck are concepts that often creep into Christian thinking. But the Bible does not portray a world governed by such forces. Instead, it teaches that we play an active part in the accomplishment of God's will. The Bible also teaches that God engages his people in prayer. For example, the Lord calls us to pray lest we fall into temptation (see Matthew 26:41). We are not helpless victims of inner drives or external forces. We can stand against them through prayer. Even when confronted with sin and judgment, we are exhorted to continue praying until God fulfills his purposes.

When asked why he prayed, David said, "Perhaps the Lord will be gracious" (2 Samuel 12:22). David had a deep sense that God is gracious above all else. He thought the Lord might relent—and he was not rebuked for praying and hoping that such would happen. On the other hand, when the Lord carried through with his judgment, David was not bitter. He knew that God was just and merciful. He knew that God's justice, more often than not, was an expression of his mercy. For David and Bathsheba, judgment was accompanied by the mercy of a second child:

> Then David comforted Bathsheba, his wife, and slept with her. She became pregnant and gave birth to a son, and they named him Solomon. The Lord loved the child and sent word through Nathan the prophet that his name should be Jedidiah—"beloved of the Lord"—because the Lord loved him. (2 Samuel 12:24-25)

The Lord gave David and Bathsheba another child, Solomon, who became the next great king of Israel—and an expression of God's grace.

TRUTH AND CONSEQUENCES

While God's grace and forgiveness are real, repentance doesn't necessarily kill the seeds of consequences, as we learn in Galatians 6:7-8: "Don't be misled. Remember that you can't ignore God and get away with it. You will always reap what you sow! Those who live only to satisfy their own sinful desires will harvest the consequences of decay and death. But those who live to please the Spirit will harvest everlasting life from the Spirit." As the saying goes, *you can't sow your wild oats on Saturday night and pray for a crop failure on Sunday morning!*

Sin and its consequences have to be viewed on two levels: On the spiritual level, sin means broken relationships—with God and others. Relationship with God is restored by repentance and confession. But on the human level, confession and forgiveness don't reverse the natural consequences of sin. The eternal judgment may be removed and the spiritual relationship restored, but the temporal consequences remain.

The consequence of David and Bathsheba's sin was that the nation would never again be the same. Sin's taint continued to plague David's dynasty. David's daughter Tamar was raped by his son Amnon. Amnon was then killed by Tamar's brother Absalom. Absalom was exiled but later returned, only to lead a rebellion against his father, David. David's son Solomon was eventually led astray by his marriages, and the threat of the sword reemerged at his death through the rebellion of Jeroboam.

MOVING INTO ACCEPTANCE

We may question God's judgment, resent it, deny it, or accept it. Once forced to come to terms with it, David accepted it. He didn't resign himself to "fate" but engaged God through prayer. Then, with a maturity we must admire despite his past behavior, he submitted himself to God's judgment and reengaged in life. Second Samuel 12:23 is a powerful statement of the reality David finally faced: "But why should I fast when he is dead? Can I bring him back again? I will go to him one day, but he cannot return to me."

Judgment need not separate us from the Lord. In fact, it can be the means of restoration. I know of a man who was caught embezzling funds from his business. Being caught cost him his job and meant he would have to repay a negotiated amount. He said he felt as if he had fallen under a kind of "spell" in which he had drifted from God and no longer felt any guilt for his sin. "When I got caught," he said, "it was like someone shook me awake from a nightmare. I'm glad I'm finally awake, but it isn't going to be easy or pleasant getting through all this!" This man accepted the consequences of his wrong behavior, including the need to make restitution. He knew he was forgiven, but he also knew he had to make things right.

SEARCHING THE SOUL

There was more to David's prayer than praying for his child. David was searching his own heart, coming to terms with his lapse in obedience, trying to understand the significance of God's judgment. Let's look more closely at these ideas.

First, David was searching his own heart. We see a clear profession of this in another prayer of David:

> *Search me, O God, and know my heart;*
> *test me and know my thoughts.*
> *Point out anything in me that offends you,*
> *and lead me along the path of everlasting life.*
>   *(Psalm 139:23-24)*

Prayer exposes us. When we come honestly into the presence of the light, the darkness is driven back. We begin to see ourselves from God's perspective. We confront the mixed motives, vulnerabilities, presumption, carelessness, wounds, and fears that drive us. The purpose of our searching prayer shouldn't be self-condemnation but restoration and change. God is in the business of changing our heart and often uses prayer to do it.

I believe that, in the process of searching his heart, David was pondering God's judgment. The Bible is silent on this point, but I surmise that David considered God's earlier promise, delivered by Nathan the prophet, of establishing David's holy dynasty:

> And now the Lord declares that he will build a house for you—a dynasty of kings! For when you die, I will raise up one of your descendants, and I will make his kingdom strong. He is the one who

will build a house—a temple—for my name. And
I will establish the throne of his kingdom forever.
I will be his father, and he will be my son. If he
sins, I will use other nations to punish him. But
my unfailing love will not be taken from him as
I took it from Saul, whom I removed before you.
Your dynasty and your kingdom will continue
for all time before me, and your throne will be
secure forever. (2 Samuel 7:11-16)

This passage is a clue to understanding the harsh judgment visited upon David and Bathsheba. For reasons we cannot claim to fully understand, God chose to allow the newborn child to die. Perhaps the child jeopardized the continuation of the messianic dynasty. In any case, David had to learn that the promise of God is not a license to ignore the command of God. Some of God's blessings are clearly conditional. We cannot arrogantly spurn the way of obedience in the name of grace! As Dietrich Bonhoeffer pointed out, grace is free, but it is not cheap.[2]

WHAT DOES IT ALL MEAN?

If it seems that God isn't answering your prayers, how can you know if it's a result of God's judgment? Could it be that you are like David, guilty of sin but clueless about your culpability? Or are you like Sherry, innocent but suffering from false guilt? Or are you perhaps wrongly associating a specific sin with unanswered prayer because of misplaced guilt? How can you determine if God's judgment is involved in your situation?

TAKING A MORE CAREFUL LOOK AT JUDGMENT

Earlier in this chapter, I urged you not to jump to the conclusion that unanswered prayer is the result of sin. In fact, I'd suggest that, unless you know there is willful sin in your life, you should assume that your suffering has nothing to do with any wrongdoing on your part. Of course, given the human capacity for self-deception, it's helpful to get counsel about the possibility of unacknowledged sin. A more mature Christian, a "Nathan," may be able to help you discern the truth. But unless you've been confronted by a "Nathan," be extremely cautious about concluding that your unanswered prayer is evidence of God's judgment.

Remember, too, that judgment isn't like a lottery. God doesn't just pick a sin committed by some poor loser and then drop a random punishment on him. The judgments in the Bible are related directly to particular sins. In the time of King Ahab and the prophet Elijah, God judged Israel for worshiping Baal, the Canaanite god of fertility. What better judgment could God send than drought, proving Baal impotent over the weather? (See 1 Kings 17–19.) When Israel sought military alliances apart from God's direction, God judged the nation through overwhelming military defeat (see 2 Chronicles 18). The Bible reveals that there is usually a cause-and-effect process at work by which sin is judged in a way appropriate to it. As the old saying goes, let the punishment fit the crime. So be cautious about concluding that a difficulty in one area of life is the consequence of sin in another.

Then there's the plain fact that we are never good enough to deserve any answered prayers. If our worthiness were the criterion God used to grant our requests, we'd never get any positive response from the Lord! Apart from Christ, we are all unworthy to merit God's blessings. That may sound harsh, but it is the clear teaching of God's Word.

I recall hearing of a pastor who preached a scathing sermon on original sin. He described in vivid detail the scandal of sin and the perversity of the human heart. The pastor decried all claims of virtue and declared in no uncertain terms that we are all sinners, worthy of damnation apart from Christ. After the message, a woman walked up to the pastor. Holding her thumb and forefinger just barely apart, she said, "Pastor, you made me feel this small!"

"That's too much!" he exclaimed. "Too much!"

Hard as it is to accept, this is the biblical view of humanity. "None is righteous, no, not one" (Romans 3:10, RSV). "For all have sinned and fall short of the glory of God" (Romans 3:23, NIV). If God only answered when we were "worthy," he would be contradicting his own gospel of grace. Even in Christ, we cannot claim merit as the basis for our prayers being answered.

So what are we to conclude?

First, that all answered prayer is a gift, an expression of God's grace and love. Unanswered prayers do not negate God's love.

Second, that not all our unanswered prayers are the result of our sins.

Third, that when God does judge, his judgment

makes sense—that is, the judgment is linked in some way to the sin. God does not visit suffering and judgment randomly on his people.

IS THIS WHY MY PRAYER IS STILL UNANSWERED?

Is God withholding an answer to your prayer because he is judging your sin? Unless you've been confronted by a "Nathan," I again encourage you to tread this matter with the utmost care. As you consider whether or not you are under judgment, it is wise to seek counsel from a more mature Christian who can help you discern the truth. Without a direct word from God through a personal "prophet Nathan," you should be extremely cautious about concluding that your unanswered prayer—or any other person's unanswered prayer—is evidence of God's judgment.

HOW TO PRAY

Pray for a soft heart, for a willingness to be exposed and vulnerable. It is the only hope of healing. This may be a time for courageous soul-searching. For praying the words of Psalm 139. For inviting the Lord to search your heart and expose any sin that may be blocking full fellowship with the Lord and preventing any answer to prayer.

If something is revealed, deal with the particular sin. Confess, repent, make amends, or make restitution. Get right with God, and then look at your prayer in a new light.

It may be that your situation is like David's. God's

judgment may be exercised, and you are left with the task of acceptance. Examine again David's response as he yielded humbly to the Lord.

If no particular sin is revealed, commit yourself to the continual pursuit of holiness, realizing that you may not recognize your sin. We all have hidden faults as we are told several times in Scripture. David himself writes in Psalm 19:12-13 (NIV):

> *Who can discern his errors?*
> *Forgive my hidden faults.*
> *Keep your servant also from willful sins;*
> *may they not rule over me.*

Paul also said he was unable to judge himself fully (see 1 Corinthians 4:3-4) but trusted himself to God's grace. It's important that we repent and release known sin—and refuse to be shackled by false or misplaced guilt.

Getting right with the Lord is the first and primary concern of our life. In the end, what we most desire is not the answer to our prayer, but fellowship with the one who is the Answer to all of life.

NOTES

1. Douglas J. Rumford, *SoulShaping* (Wheaton, Ill.: Tyndale House Publishers, Inc., 1996), 136.

2. Dietrich Bonhoeffer, *The Cost of Discipleship* (New York: The Macmillan Company, 1959), 45–60.

CHAPTER THREE

The Principle of Mystery

Donna had been struggling with a serious infection for over a year. Having been far from faith prior to her illness, she started coming back to church. At one church she attended she heard the pastor say, "People who live in sin or unforgiveness are the only ones who don't receive healing." That statement only made her feel more sick and discouraged. Her poor health didn't result from immoral activity. To the best of her knowledge there were no significant grudges or alienated relationships in her life. Yet the preacher was saying that her continuing illness was her own fault. It was a message that sent Donna into a deepening spiral of depression.

One of our church members, Margaret, was Donna's neighbor. After listening to her struggles one day, Margaret gave Donna a copy of a tape I had preached on unanswered prayer. In a note back to Margaret, Donna wrote, "I have been so discouraged at times that I've considered ending my life. It wasn't until I heard the tape on unanswered prayer that I gained hope." Donna gave our church a try. Her first Sunday I was preaching on "Breaking Free from Depression." "I could hardly believe that you preached on that subject," she told me later. "It was like God was saying, 'Donna, have hope. You're gonna get through this.'"

Donna is still dealing with her physical illness, but her soul is reviving. "Even though I still don't know when I'll get better, knowing that God is with me is making all the difference," she said. Donna is learning to live with the mystery of her illness and her unanswered prayer.

MYSTERY IS A FACT OF LIFE

The very word *mystery* sparks curiosity and fascination. We are intrigued by murder mysteries in books and on television and by real-life mysteries such as the assassinations of President John F. Kennedy and Martin Luther King Jr. or the death of actress Marilyn Monroe. As of this writing, these are still unsolved puzzles. Because of lack of information, lack of forensic ability, lack of resources, or the basic fact that we cannot turn back the clock and observe certain events, we may never have the answers to these mysteries.

When it comes to unanswered prayer, we are exploring a different type of mystery, one based on simple mortality. As finite creatures, we are incapable of understanding the mind and ways of God.

William Cowper was regarded by many as the leading English poet of his day. He was especially noted for his translation of Homer in 1791. Cowper suffered severe periods of depression throughout his life, the worst at age thirty-two. His despair was so great that he decided to end his life. He took what he thought was a lethal dose of laudanum (a tincture of opium) but did not succeed. So he hired a horse-drawn carriage to take him to the Thames River, where he intended to throw himself off the bridge. It was one of London's foggiest nights. The driver drove for an hour without reaching the bridge. Frustrated, Cowper decided to get out and walk to the bridge. But he found to his surprise they had actually gone in a circle and he was back at his own doorstep!

The next morning he attempted to kill himself by falling on a knife, but the blade broke and his life was spared. He then tried to hang himself and was cut down—unconscious but still alive. Then one morning, on an impulse, he took up his Bible and read a verse in the letter to the Romans. In a moment he received strength to believe and rejoiced in the forgiving power of God. Sometime later, Cowper summed up his faith in God's loving manner of dealing with him in a great hymn that became a favorite among Christians:

> God moves in a mysterious way
> His wonders to perform;
> He plants His footsteps in the sea,
> And rides upon the storm.
>
> Deep in unfathomable mines
> Of never-failing skill,
> He treasures up His bright designs,
> And works His sovereign will.

Ye fearful saints, fresh courage take;.
The clouds ye so much dread
Are big with mercy, and shall break
With blessing on your head.

Judge not the Lord by feeble sense,
But trust Him for His grace;
Behind a frowning providence
He hides a smiling face.

His purposes will ripen fast,
Unfolding every hour;
The bud may have a bitter taste,
But sweet will be the flower.

Blind unbelief is sure to err,
And scan His work in vain;
God is His own interpreter,
And He will make it plain. [1]

For many of us, the veil of mystery remains firmly drawn over our prayer requests. This is difficult, especially when our requests seem so good, so proper, so right.

I know of a pastor who, despite his faithful work, was facing increasing conflict in his church. Many of us joined him in praying that the conflict would be resolved and that the ministry would flourish. Only a few church members were stirring up the discord, but somehow they gained control. Eventually, this pastor was cruelly driven out of his church. Why? It's a mystery.

I know a man whose brother was found dead. There was no evidence of foul play or suicide, but at age twenty-seven, he was gone. His family has prayed and prayed for the answer to this tragedy. But none is forthcoming. It's a mystery.

I know a family whose house was destroyed by apparent arson. Family members have prayed and prayed for the cause to be determined and any guilty party to be apprehended, but the case has been filed as unsolved. It's a mystery.

Unresolved tragedies such as these are disconcerting, disquieting, and even doubt inducing. Unless we learn how to live with them, they can erode our joy and our confidence in God.

THERE'S SO MUCH WE CAN'T UNDERSTAND

Mystery is a central characteristic of the spiritual life. This is presented most clearly in Isaiah 55:8-9: "My thoughts are completely different from yours," says the Lord. "And my ways are far beyond anything you could imagine. For just as the heavens are higher than the earth, so are my ways higher than your ways and my thoughts higher than your thoughts."

We are finite. The simple fact that we are human means that there is a limit to our understanding. God's thoughts are not our thoughts. We cannot discern the long-term, even eternal, ramifications of our requests. We cannot understand the intricate web of relationships and events that may be blocking the answer we desire. We cannot discern how a delay in answering our prayers may actually be preparing us for a much greater manifestation of God's grace and power. In short, we have to trust God and seek to see life from the eternal perspective. God may say no for reasons we may never understand this side of heaven. In the process, he may supply things we didn't even know we needed or protect us from dangers we did not perceive.

David often conveyed a sense of awe at the mystery of life. In a simple but profound image he writes:

> Lord, my heart is not proud;
> my eyes are not haughty.
> I don't concern myself with matters too great
>   or awesome for me.
> But I have stilled and quieted myself,
> just as a small child is quiet with its mother.
> Yes, like a small child is my soul within me.
> O Israel, put your hope in the Lord—
> now and always.
>   (Psalm 131:1-3)

My wife, Sarah, and I have gained some insight into mystery in our role as parents. Wanting to be fair, we used to try to keep everything absolutely even in terms of the amount of time, attention, and financial support we gave our children. But we've discovered that each child has had different needs at different times. We have had to respond to these needs differently. Things haven't always evened out—at least not yet. The "unequal" treatment makes sense from our point of view as parents but not always from theirs as children. I can only say to them, "When you are a parent, this may make sense to you. Please trust me that I have your best interests at heart."

Sometimes I feel that God is giving me unequal treatment. But I have begun to hear him saying to me about certain issues, "Doug, since you'll never be God, this may never make sense to you. Trust me—I have your best interests at heart."

We are not only finite but fallen. Our mind and outlook are still deeply influenced by sin. We cannot fully comprehend how much the tint of sin shades everything. In fact, we sometimes cannot understand our own heart or behavior. Paul describes this most vividly in his letter to the Romans:

> I don't understand myself at all, for I really want to do what is right, but I don't do it. Instead, I do the very thing I hate. I know perfectly well that what I am doing is wrong, and my bad conscience shows that I agree that the law is good. But I can't help myself, because it is sin inside me that makes me do these evil things.
>
> I know I am rotten through and through so far as my old sinful nature is concerned. No matter which way I turn, I can't make myself do right. I want to, but I can't. When I want to do good, I don't. And when I try not to do wrong, I do it anyway. But if I am doing what I don't want to do, I am not really the one doing it; the sin within me is doing it. (Romans 7:15-20)

If we cannot understand ourselves, how are we to understand the ways of a holy, infinite God?

God's love is based on his commitment to us, not on our performance. This is what the psalmist means when he says, "As a father has compassion on his children, so the Lord has compassion on those who fear him; for he knows how we are formed, he remembers that we are dust (Psalm 103:13-14, NIV).

We are finite and fallen, but not hopeless. These facts can bring us some sense of greater patience with God and with ourselves in times of waiting and confusion.

WE THINK WE KNOW BEST

"It makes sense to me. Why can't God see it?" This is often our first impatient reaction as we wait for an answer to a request. But we don't know all the facts.

It might seem to make sense to give a person a certain medicine for a problem. But it may be that the medicine would cause side effects that we don't know about.

It might seem best to bring a person to faith. But it may be that a lasting change is going to require a more thorough breaking. The seed that falls among the thorns will soon choke.

It might seem reasonable to expect big numbers in church growth, but it may be that many would never get beyond superficial faith without the often-slow process of developing church leadership and a vision for discipleship.

It might seem to make sense for God to provide abundant financial resources, but it may be that too much money could compromise our witness and commitment.

We think we know best, but sometimes we don't have all the facts. Consider the mysteries of Jesus' life and ministry strategy. *Why was he born in an obscure village? Why did he wait so long to begin his work? Why did he choose only twelve disciples? Why did he live such a short life? Why did he leave a town where things were going so well in order to go elsewhere?* We might have planned things differently, but God knows best.

Think of the mysteries embedded in Jesus' teaching: *Give up your life to gain it. Give in order to receive. Turn the other cheek.* To the world—and often to us—these teachings just don't make sense. But God's thoughts are not our thoughts, and God's ways are not our ways. Certainly there is enough evidence to convince us that apparent solutions are not always answers and that apparent problems are not always the obstacles we thought they were.

EVEN JESUS HAD UNANSWERED PRAYER

As Philip Yancey pointed out in a fascinating article in *Christianity Today*, even Jesus' prayers weren't all answered! There were at least three unanswered prayers in Jesus' life and ministry.[2] The first concerns Jesus' prayer in selecting his disciples. How do you think Jesus prayed when he went up on the mountain and prayed all night for his closest followers? I would imagine his prayer went something like this: "O God, give me godly men who will be faithful throughout their life. Give me men who will understand and receive this word." How was his prayer answered? Jesus selected twelve disciples. One of them was Judas.

Think of Jesus in the Garden of Gethsemane, praying for the cup of suffering to pass from him. His prayer for that particular deliverance was not answered. Shortly thereafter, he was sent to the cross.

Perhaps the most poignant of Jesus' unanswered prayers was his prayer for the church. As told in John 17:21, Jesus prayed, "My prayer for all of them is that they will be one, just as you and I are one, Father—that just as you are in me and I am in you, so they will be in us, and the world will believe you sent me."

That prayer for unity has not been answered for two thousand years. Even Jesus, interceding at the right hand of God, has longings in his heart that have not yet been fulfilled. This is a mystery.

P. T. Forsyth, the British theologian and preacher, made this profound observation: "We shall come one day to a heaven where we shall gratefully know that God's refusals were sometimes the true answer to our truest prayers."[3] The point is to trust God's heart even when we cannot read his mind.

IS THIS WHY MY PRAYER IS STILL UNANSWERED?

If you can discern no other reason for your unanswered prayer, then it may be that you are simply in a time of mystery—one that may last for a brief season or for a lifetime. But it need not stop your prayers nor weaken your faith.

HOW TO PRAY IN LIGHT OF MYSTERY

In the midst of mystery, we have three primary needs: for assurance of God's love, for faith in his wisdom, and for strength to endure. Make these the focus of your prayer.

Cultivate love. A period of waiting can be a time of learning to want God himself above anything God may be able to give you.

Cultivate faith. Trust God's heart even when you cannot read his mind. Tell yourself that though you cannot see the outcome, you can trust the Lord to do the best thing. Faith has more to do with your relationship with the Lord than with the ticking of a clock. Let God be God. "When it comes to accomplishing things for God, you will find that high aspirations, enthusiastic feelings, careful planning and being able to express yourself well are not worth very much. The important thing is absolute surrender to God. You can do anything He wants you to do if you are walking in the light of full surrender."[4]

The plain fact is that there are so many things we cannot know, and if we did know, wouldn't understand, and if we did understand, wouldn't agree with!

Cultivate hope. Hope generates strength, awakening the will to endure. We all know the experience of seeing a finish line and finding a second wind. It's the kind of response that occurs when we place our confidence in the Lord rather than in our ability to explain or reason.

It's possible to find hope in mystery. When you accept the mystery, you learn to rest in the Lord, to want him more than you want your answer, to release the anxiety and burden to him. Mystery builds faith, not as a means of escaping responsibility, but as a way of casting yourself on the Lord.

In addition to cultivating love, faith, and the hope that generates strength, there are several other principles that can enrich your prayer and sustain your faith:

Cultivate humility. Waiting is one of God's tools for learning humility. As you wait, confess and forsake pride and self-seeking. Seek to honor God above all else.

Cultivate acceptance. Let go of your agenda and trust God to give you what is best. Consider the difference between resignation and acceptance. Resignation is a discouraged giving in to fatalism. It's an "Oh well . . ." attitude. Acceptance is an affirmation of God's love and care, an expression of trust in what you cannot yet understand.

Search God's Word. God's thoughts are not ours, and his Word is always fruitful: "The rain and snow come down from the heavens and stay on the ground to water the earth. They cause the grain to grow, producing seed for the farmer and bread for the hungry. It is the same with my word. I send it out, and it always produces fruit. It will accomplish all I want it to, and it will prosper everywhere I send it" (Isaiah 55:10-13).

Reading God's Word is the nearest thing to reading his mind! When you are stuck, when you are perplexed, you can always turn to his Word. Read it with this prayer: *Holy Spirit, open my mind and heart to the mind of Christ* (see 1 Corinthians 2:16).

I don't quote poetry very often, but the following poem powerfully expresses the qualities that can be developed in us by waiting through a time of mystery. The author points out that we may only get clues about a mystery, but we may still discover qualities and experiences of God that could come no other way.

Child, You Must Wait

Desperately, helplessly, longingly I cried;
Quietly, patiently, lovingly God replied.
I plead and I wept for a clue to my fate,
And the Master so gently said, "Child, you must wait."

"Wait? You say wait!" My indignant reply.
"Lord, I need answers, I need to know why!
Is your hand shortened? Or have you not heard?
By faith, I have asked, and am claiming your word.

"My future and all to which I can relate,
Hangs in the balance and you tell me to wait?
I'm needing a 'Yes,' a go-ahead sign.
Or even a 'No,' to which I can resign.

"And Lord, you promised that if we believe,
We need but ask, and we shall receive.
And Lord, I've been asking, and this is my cry:
'I'm weary of asking! I need a reply.'"

Then quietly, softly, I learned of my fate.
As my Master replied once again, "You must wait."
So, I slumped in my chair, defeated and taut.
And grumbled to God, "So, I'm waiting . . . for what?"

He seemed, then, to kneel, and his eyes wept with mine.
And He tenderly said, "I could give you a sign.
I could shake the heavens, and darken the sun.
I could raise the dead, and cause mountains to run.

"All you seek I could give, and pleased you would be.
You would have what you want—But, you wouldn't know
*   me.*
You'd not know the depth of my love for each saint.
You'd not know the power that I give to the faint.

"You'd not learn to see through the clouds of despair;
You'd not learn to trust just by knowing I'm there.
You'd not know the joy of resting in me.
When darkness and silence were all you could see.

"You'd never experience that fullness of love
As the peace of my Spirit descends like a dove.
You'd know what I give and I save . . . (For a start),
But you'd not know the depth of the beat of my heart.

"The glow of my comfort late into the night,
The faith that I give when you walk without sight.
The depth that's beyond getting just what you asked
Of an infinite God, who makes what you have last.

"You'd never know, should your pain quickly flee,
What it means that 'my grace is sufficient for Thee.'
Yes, your dreams for your loved ones overnight would come
    true.
But, oh, the loss if I lost . . . What I'm doing in you!

"So, be silent, my child, and in time you will see,
That the greatest of gifts is to get to know me.
And though oft' may my answers seem terribly late.
My most precious answer of all is still, 'Wait.'"

Author unknown

By God's grace, your time of waiting may actually both lessen and deepen the mystery of faith.

NOTES

1. Quoted from *The One Year Book of Hymns* (Wheaton, Ill.:, Tyndale House Publishers, Inc., 1995), January 22.

2. Philip Yancey, "Jesus' Unanswered Prayers," *Christianity Today* (9 February 1998): 152.

3. P. T. Forsyth, *The Soul of Prayer* (Grand Rapids: William B. Eerdmans Publishing Company, 1916), 14. Cited in Richard Foster, *Prayer* (San Francisco: Harper San Francisco, 1992), 180–81.

4. Francois Fenelon, *Let Go* (New Kensington, Pa.: Whitaker House, 1973), 35.

CHAPTER FOUR

The Principle of Spiritual Warfare

Pastor Jim was an earnest, faithful pastor. He knew there were problems when he came to his new congregation but felt convinced of God's call, a call that was affirmed by a large majority of the members. As hard as he worked, however, parishioners were unresponsive to his preaching and ministry. They weren't antagonistic, and there was little conflict, but nothing spiritual was taking hold. Jim and his wife, Brenda, prayed and prayed. They asked some spiritually mature congregational leaders to join them in prayer. Still, there was no spiritual vitality stirring in the church. For some time, Jim questioned his abilities and even sent sermon tapes to his seminary preaching professor for comment. His professor was very positive about his messages and offered little in the way of advice or criticism. Then a missionary couple whom the church had supported for a number of years came to visit. In the course of personal conversations with them, Jim's frustrations and deep concern came to light.

"We think there is something else going on," said John.

"We have been praying for you and for this congregation for a number of years and have a strong sense that there is a spiritual block here," said John's wife, Gayle.

Jim was confused by what John and Gayle were telling him. These were credible, spiritually mature people, yet they were saying that their prayers weren't getting through because of some evil or demonic interference. Jim had no theological frame of reference for understanding such interference.

John and Gayle asked if Jim and Brenda and some of their most mature church leaders would be willing to go as a group through the entire church facility, consecrating it to the Lord and "cleaning out the evil garbage."

Some quick phone calls produced a small group who gathered at the church Sunday afternoon. The turning point came when they were in the youth room. They began to pray, but Gayle interrupted. She felt strongly that the Lord was telling her there had been an occult experience—something involving a Ouija board—in the room.

One of the church leaders, Harlan, spoke up. "How could you know that?"

"I don't know how," said Gayle. "It just came to me. I don't see how I could know, apart from the Holy Spirit's telling me. Is there something you know about this?"

"Well, about twenty-five years ago," said Harlan, "we had a couple working with our junior and senior high kids. They were fairly new, but they were the nicest people. At first things seemed great—you know how hard it is to get youth advisers! But then they had a huge Halloween party. They had the kids play some very unusual games, along the lines of séances, Ouija boards, and guessing games with those 'Magic Eight Balls.' When word got to us on the church board, we were very concerned. We wanted to confront them and ask them to step down, but the pastor encouraged us to leave them alone. He said he'd talk to them and asked us to keep it completely confidential. I have never said a word of this to anybody. I'm not really sure what happened, but the couple left shortly after the pastor did a year or so later."

The group prayed earnestly, renouncing the evil that had been welcomed into that room and praying for the Holy Spirit to cleanse it and fill it completely. They then continued throughout the church facilities.

"It was such a blessing just to have an intense, focused time of prayer for this ministry," Jim told me, "but what happened in the youth room really opened my eyes. It was like I could feel a blanket of darkness lifting. I felt physically lighter as we prayed."

And what happened in the church? Spiritual interest began to stir. People seemed to be able to hear the truth of God's Word in a way that they hadn't before. The turnaround wasn't dramatic, but it began a quiet, persistent renewal that continues today. Pastor Jim believes it might not have happened if he and his church leaders hadn't engaged in spiritual warfare with the forces of evil.

TAKING EVIL SERIOUSLY

I have always had complete faith that God's Word is to-
tally true and trustworthy. And I have always believed in
the reality of personal evil in the form of the devil and
demons. But I confess to having lived in a state of practical unbelief about the active presence and manifestation of evil. I have been more of a "naturalist" rather
than a "supernaturalist" when it comes to spiritual warfare. Looking back, I realize that I had limited the concept of spiritual warfare to temptations, to the battle
against rational arguments that threatened the faith,
and to social and political systems that oppress people.
But the time came when I was confronted, like Pastor
Jim, with more significant expressions of evil (the story
of how this happened is explained more fully in my
book *What about Spiritual Warfare?*). I heard about things I
didn't understand. I witnessed circumstances that
couldn't be explained in terms of "normal" experience. I was faced with the fact that evil was far more real
and tangible than I had expected.

No discussion of unanswered prayer would be complete without examining the fact that God's enemies are
trying to block both our prayers and God's answers.
Spiritual warfare is a way of life for Jesus' followers. Far
from making us immune to temptation, spiritual
growth stirs spiritual opposition. Scripture abounds
with accounts of spiritual warfare: From the Garden of
Eden to the court of Pharaoh, from Jesus' experience in
the wilderness to Paul's encounters with demons in

Acts, we see that there is an invisible world set in opposition to the kingdom of God.

THE REALITY OF SPIRITUAL WARFARE

When Daniel was eighty years old, still living in Babylon
even though the Jews had been allowed by Cyrus to return to their homeland, he had his final vision. It was a
vision of war and great hardship, a vision that caused
him to mourn for weeks. Then a heavenly messenger
appeared to him:

> Then he [the angel] said, "Don't be afraid,
> Daniel. Since the first day you began to pray for
> understanding and to humble yourself before
> your God, your request has been heard in
> heaven. I have come in answer to your prayer.
> But for twenty-one days the spirit prince of
> the kingdom of Persia blocked my way. Then
> Michael, one of the archangels, came to help me,
> and I left him there with the spirit prince of the
> kingdom of Persia. Now I am here to explain
> what will happen to your people in the future, for
> this vision concerns a time yet to come." (Daniel
> 10:12-14)

This is an intriguing account of a delayed answer to
prayer caused by evil's interference. What fascinates me
most about this passage is that, while God heard Daniel's prayer immediately, evil forces were able to keep
the answer from Daniel for twenty-one days. I want to

be careful not to draw too many conclusions from such a difficult passage. And I won't attempt to explain here the concept of territorial spirits that are thought to be assigned to particular geographic areas. Nevertheless, the picture of demonic interference is consistent with the rest of Scripture. When Jesus was in the wilderness, for example, the devil intruded, disrupting his prayers. What we learn from these passages and others in the Bible is this: The evil one interferes with communication between God and his people.

JAMMING THE SIGNAL

When I was in elementary school, I used to listen to my parents' old shortwave radio. My friend Billy and I liked to pick up international broadcasts and write for postcards from stations around the world. As we would turn the dial, we would hear stations in South America and Europe. Then we'd hear this awful buzzing sound, different from the normal static. "That's the Russians!" said Billy, "They're jamming the broadcasts of American stations." I never understood the technology, but I got the point: It's one thing to broadcast but another thing to get through. Strong forces can block communication.

Novelist Frank Peretti portrays the nature of "spiritual jamming" in his books *This Present Darkness* and *Piercing the Darkness.* Peretti tells his stories on two levels, with the human plot mirrored by a plot depicting the battle between the righteous hosts of God and the demonic hosts of evil. It is a very effective portrayal of the "war in the heavens" that is continually waged. While we must be careful about taking Peretti's stories literally, we can learn a great deal from them about the existence of spiritual warfare and the overcoming power of persistent prayer.

If you have never thought of these things or find them difficult to believe, I encourage you to be open to what follows, to search the Bible and to trust the Lord to make things clear.

GOD'S ENEMY IS OUR ENEMY TOO

One of the best ways to hurt God is to hurt those whom God loves. So the evil one goes after us, tempting us as Adam and Eve were tempted in the Garden of Eden and as Jesus was tempted in the wilderness. And we may not have any idea what lies behind our problems. The story of Job vividly illustrates that there are spiritual dynamics going on around us that we can never understand apart from revelation (see Job 2:1-10).

When we pray, we enter into the spiritual dimension. We step onto the battlefield between God and evil. Ephesians 6:12 reminds us: "For we are not fighting against people made of flesh and blood, but against the evil rulers and authorities of the unseen world, against those mighty powers of darkness who rule this world, and against wicked spirits in the heavenly realms."

IS THIS WHY MY PRAYER IS STILL UNANSWERED?

It's difficult to discern whether or not spiritual warfare is the factor inhibiting your prayer, especially if, like

Pastor Jim, you've never faced this kind of thing before. But be encouraged: Daniel, the wise old prophet of God, didn't realize that a spiritual battle was delaying the answer to his prayers until he was informed by an angel. And Daniel's continued prayer brought victory, despite the fact that he didn't immediately recognize the source of the problem. Still, there are steps we can take in examining our prayers. They fall under the heading of discernment.

DISCERNING A SPIRITUAL BLOCK

I encourage you to follow a basic inventory when trying to discern whether or not a prayer is blocked because of spiritual warfare:

First, test to see if the situation can best be explained by the more "natural" or "common" reasons for unanswered prayer as discussed in other chapters:

> God's timing and progressive victory
> Our sin and the principle of judgment
> God's prerogative and the principle of mystery
> God's honor and the principle of preparation
> Our pride and the principle of selfishness

Second, search the past for potential sources of current spiritual blockage. Have you been involved with any occult practices? Is there any evidence or memory of occult practices related to your prayer situation? If so, this in itself could be a major reason for prayer interference. Stop all these practices immediately and renounce them. If you haven't been personally involved but are aware that such practices have occurred, you can be confident in your authority in Christ to address the situation. Remember the promise of 1 John 4:4, "For he who is in you is greater than he who is in the world" (RSV). If you know of people who are indulging in such practices, you must determine their receptivity to spiritual correction. You may be able to confront them, warning them of the dangers of the occult. If they are unreceptive, you must break away from fellowship with them. No matter what, have a spiritually mature friend, pastor, or counselor pray with you, because occult practices can be strongholds of the evil one. One helpful resource that offers specific prayers for breaking free from evil is Neil T. Anderson's book *The Bondage Breaker*.

Third, ask God to reveal the source of the problem. In the example at the beginning of the chapter, Gayle prayed for specific direction. She had begun with a "sense," a vague but persistent feeling that there was a spiritual warfare problem. Then she began to explore the area with the prayer partnership of others. This is not something you do alone! She also took time to listen to the Lord. He communicated with her through a picture (not a vision) that was confirmed by another person. Once they had this insight, they were able to pray with power and authority.

The Bible teaches that there are three sources of spiritual opposition: the world, the flesh, and the devil. When we have earnestly checked the world and the flesh and are still faced with strong opposition, we are likely dealing with a matter of spiritual interference.

HOW TO PRAY

Here are some basic principles for praying when dealing with spiritual interference (for a more thorough treatment of this subject, see my book *What about Spiritual Warfare?*):

Get support from spiritually mature friends for both the process of discernment as well as for your own spiritual protection. An isolated person is the devil's favorite target. The hosts of evil find it far more difficult to attack a community of faith and love. A word of warning: You may need to pray about whom to choose for this process. People are increasingly open to this concept of prayer, but you should not assume that everyone is on the same page. You may want to ask people what they think about spiritual warfare before you disclose your particular need.

Confess and repent of any known sin in your life. Dark forces are like rats, feeding on garbage. Our sins are like spiritual garbage.

Release any hurt in your life. Our wounds can also be openings for evil. Lingering hurts, grudges, bitterness, discouragement, and self-condemnation can all fuel evil forces. That's one of the reasons Paul exhorts us, "And 'don't sin by letting anger gain control over you.' Don't let the sun go down while you are still angry, for anger gives a mighty foothold to the Devil" (Ephesians 4:26-27).

Maintain discipline in prayer. Daniel's life demonstrated the power of persistent prayer, often coupled with fasting. We know that he prayed three times a day (see Daniel 6:10) and that he frequently practiced partial fasts such as the one described in Daniel 10:3: "All that time I had eaten no rich food or meat, had drunk no wine, and had used no fragrant oils."

Daniel's persistence in prayer and fasting released God's overcoming power. We often give up too quickly. Again, it was not Daniel's recognition of spiritual conflict that broke the hold of evil and brought his answer. Daniel was answered because of God's love and grace. "Then the one who looked like a man touched me again, and I felt my strength returning. 'Don't be afraid,' he said, 'for you are deeply loved by God. Be at peace; take heart and be strong!'" (Daniel 10:18-19).

Rely on the truth and power of God's Word. When Jesus faced spiritual attack in the wilderness, he answered it with Scripture (see Matthew 4).

God's Word warns of the practices that are off-limits to the people of God. Here, for example, are his instructions to the Israelites as they were preparing to enter the Promised Land:

> When you arrive in the land the Lord your God
> is giving you, be very careful not to imitate the
> detestable customs of the nations living there.
> For example, never sacrifice your son or
> daughter as a burnt offering. And do not let your
> people practice fortune-telling or sorcery, or

allow them to interpret omens, or engage in witchcraft, or cast spells, or function as mediums or psychics, or call forth the spirits of the dead. Anyone who does these things is an object of horror and disgust to the Lord. It is because the other nations have done these things that the Lord your God will drive them out ahead of you. You must be blameless before the Lord your God. The people you are about to displace consult with sorcerers and fortune-tellers, but the Lord your God forbids you to do such things. (Deuteronomy 18:9-14)

The Bible not only guides our life but exposes the lies and deceptions of evil.

Choose faith. Maybe you've heard the story about the devil's yard sale. There were numerous demonic items for sale. But one case had an item for display only that was marked "The Devil's Favorite Tool." It was discouragement. Discouragement makes way for all other temptations. It wears down the spirit, hardens the heart, cools passion for God, and drains vitality from the soul.

Wear the armor of God. Ephesians 6:10-18 gives us the essential tools to stand against spiritual attack. We are to rely on God's power. Paul uses the analogy of armor that protects the soldier in battle. Putting on God's armor involves several steps. First, put on the belt of truth. Satan is a liar and the father of lies

(John 8:44). He lays his traps through deceit and deception. Through prayer, we can discern the lies and gain strength to walk in the truth that sets—and keeps—us free.

Second, put on God's righteousness. Though there are many levels of meaning to this phrase, the primary one is that we accept that we are forgiven through faith in Jesus Christ alone. We don't wear our own medals on our chest—we wear his! This shields us against Satan's accusations of our own guilt and unworthiness.

Third, put on the shoes of the gospel of peace. Spiritual warfare doesn't intimidate us or distract us from our mission of spreading the Good News. We are not enamored with combat. Instead, we seek peace. Prayer keeps this priority in focus.

Fourth, take the full-body shield of faith to deal with the accusations and persecutions the evil one levels at you. We refuse to believe lies. We cling to the truth. Prayer gives us the eyes of faith. It keeps our vision clear when human circumstances are foggy.

Fifth, take the helmet of salvation. At the time that Paul was writing, a soldier's helmet was a primary means of identifying his army and allegiance. We belong to the Lord's army, his salvation army. Salvation has two primary meanings. The first relates to healing, as in a salve or healing ointment. Jesus Christ has healed us from the mortal wound of sin. He has restored our spiritual health. Salvation also means deliverance. We have been released from captivity to the enemy. As we wear the helmet of salvation, we acknowledge that we belong to the God who has made us whole again.

Finally, arm yourself with the sword of the Spirit, the Word of God. The sword is our only offensive weapon. As God's Word makes a home in our heart, the Holy Spirit uses it to guard and guide us at all times.

As you take on the armor of God, pray with authority. Warfare prayer is a matter of claiming authority in Christ. Animal experts tell us that a dog will chase a person who runs away from it. If it senses fear, the dog will attack. But if the would-be victim stands his ground, the dog will back down. A similar dynamic is at work in spiritual warfare. We are to stand our ground in the power of the gospel, confident in the victory of Christ. We develop confidence as we live out the truth of 1 John 4:4: "But you belong to God, my dear children. You have already won your fight with these false prophets, because the Spirit who lives in you is greater than the spirit who lives in the world."

Don't be deceived by the enemy who tries to intimidate you. Instead, claim the reality that you have been saved not only from sin but from the principalities and powers of evil.

The concept of spiritual warfare may seem frightening, but I encourage you to consider Daniel's experience one more time. For him, spiritual warfare actually became a means through which God revealed his everlasting love and overcoming power. Near the end of the biblical account we read how the angel encouraged Daniel: "Then the one who looked like a man touched me again, and I felt my strength returning. 'Don't be afraid,' he said, 'for you are deeply loved by God. Be at peace; take heart and be strong!'" (Daniel 10:18-19).

We, too, are deeply loved by God. This is the source of our peace, our courage, and our strength. No enemy can snatch us from him. Ultimately, no evil power can resist him. So wait in this confidence.

CHAPTER FIVE

The Principle of Preparation

A number of years ago, Jill went to our church's women's conference with a very heavy heart. She'd been divorced for four years, and taking care of her two young boys and working full time were taking their toll. My wife, Sarah, and another woman, Ginny, conducted a prayer time for the women on Saturday afternoon. Jill asked for prayer. Telling me the story later, Jill described how she felt that afternoon:

"I felt humiliated because of my failed marriage. But I was so sad and so desperately lonely that I wasn't sure how to carry on. I was aching for someone to care for me. It was a raw moment when I had to cry out for the Lord."

Sarah and Ginny anointed Jill's forehead with oil (according to the counsel of James 5:14) and prayed for God to give her someone really special who would be the kind of spiritual and emotional companion her heart longed for.

"I really didn't feel any different after the prayer—

except for a sense of release that now someone else was carrying the burden with me. I had reached a point where I could hardly pray about it anymore. I just needed someone else to do the praying for me, while I tried to get through the daily pressures."

Five years later Jill came up to Sarah and said, "I have to tell you how God used you to answer my prayers. Five years ago, you and Ginny prayed for me—and this past year, God brought Steve into my life." Jill went on to tell how she had tried over the years to date and attend singles' groups but without any results. Then she went to a Christian seminar about communicating with teenagers. When the speaker talked about challenges with teenage boys, Jill chuckled. A man one chair over leaned forward, smiled, and said something to her—and the rest, as they say, is history. "I mean *his* story!" said Jill.

I asked Jill what she learned from her nine years of waiting. "I learned that God knows when I am ready for the answer. Looking back now, I see that I wasn't ready for a relationship like I am now. And Steve wasn't ready either. But God knew when we'd be ready—and it's better than either of us could have ever imagined."

Not everyone has Jill's experience of waiting and then getting a hoped-for answer to prayer. Sometimes the answer isn't the expected or desired one. It's important to note, however, that Jill's burden was lifted at the time she prayed—not when she got her answer. The lesson for us is to release our problems to God and to share them with others who will pray alongside us.

Waiting and preparation are a fact of life. We often

neglect this fact, however, when it comes to prayer. We expect God to work right away, or according to our time schedule. When the answers don't come, we may need to remind ourselves that good things often take time to come together. A lasting work requires extensive preparation.

Have you ever heard of the "Peter Principle"? The concept has nothing to do with the disciple Peter. It was introduced by Laurence J. Peter, a management expert who described it as the tendency of every employee in a hierarchy to rise to his level of incompetence. Peter's point: People may, in fact, reach the limit of their capacity. Intentional effort is required to help them develop the skills and qualities necessary for success. Otherwise, they just won't be ready.

There may be a type of "Peter Principle" at work in some cases of unanswered prayer. In some situations, we may lack the capacity to handle an answer. God, in his mercy, doesn't expose us to the often-unanticipated demands of our answered prayers until he has prepared us for them. He may not want to expose us to the level of our incompetence.

When Jesus was talking to his disciples on the night of his betrayal he said, "Oh, there is so much more I want to tell you, but you can't bear it now" (John 16:12). Jesus geared his teaching to what he felt people could handle. The same principle may be applied to prayer. God's *no* may be based on our inability to handle a *yes*. God may say no until he has produced in us the capacity and character to bear lasting fruit.

DEVELOPING THE CAPACITY FOR FULFILLING GOD'S PLAN

The story of Joseph in Genesis is one of the most fascinating examples of this principle. The account begins
with a clear message that God has great things in mind
for this young man. You may recall that Joseph had two
dreams in which he, the next to youngest in the family,
became the center of attention and devotion:

> One night Joseph had a dream and promptly
> reported the details to his brothers, causing them
> to hate him even more. "Listen to this dream,"
> he announced. "We were out in the field tying up
> bundles of grain. My bundle stood up, and then
> your bundles all gathered around and bowed low
> before it!"
>
> "So you are going to be our king, are you?" his
> brothers taunted. And they hated him all the
> more for his dream and what he had said.
>
> Then Joseph had another dream and told his
> brothers about it. "Listen to this dream," he said.
> "The sun, moon, and eleven stars bowed low
> before me!"
>
> This time he told his father as well as his
> brothers, and his father rebuked him. "What do
> you mean?" his father asked. "Will your mother,
> your brothers, and I actually come and bow
> before you?" But while his brothers were jealous
> of Joseph, his father gave it some thought and
> wondered what it all meant. (Genesis 37:5-11)

But Joseph's dreams turned into nightmares. One thing after another went wrong. Rather than standing in awe of Joseph's dream prophecies, his jealous brothers decided to kill him. After a last-minute intervention by Reuben, however, they sold him as a slave to some Ishmaelites. In turn, the Ishmaelites sold him to Potiphar, an officer of Pharaoh in Egypt. At this point, we begin to see the hand of God, weaving new qualities into the fabric of Joseph's life. God began shaping Joseph for the responsibilities and circumstances foretold in his dreams. Joseph had the vision but lacked the capacity to step immediately into the responsibilities implied in his vision. God took time both to develop a place for Joseph and to develop Joseph for that place. Before God would fulfill the place he had for him, Joseph needed to develop the capacity to receive God's promises and use his gifts in humility.

DEVELOPING THE CAPACITY FOR LEADERSHIP AND PRACTICAL ADMINISTRATION

In Potiphar's household, Joseph was given the opportunity to practice administrative leadership, working his way up the ranks to top household manager. We can imagine that Joseph learned how to manage the other servants, to plan for entertaining great numbers of guests, to order food and drink, to prepare supplies for a journey, and to oversee the manifold needs of an important military leader and his family. Though he was technically a slave, he was given a position of responsibility and honor—one that prepared him for even greater responsibility and honor.

DEVELOPING THE CAPACITY TO MAINTAIN INTEGRITY IN THE MIDST OF TEMPTATIONS

Just when it looked like things had really changed for Joseph, something happened to put him back into trouble and seemingly further from the fulfillment of his God-given dreams. In the process of managing Potiphar's household, he attracted the attention of Potiphar's wife. She had more than housekeeping in mind! When Joseph refused her advances, she accused him of rape, and he was sent to prison. It must have looked to Joseph like yet another step backward, away from the fulfillment of his dreams. Little did he know that he would be faced with far greater temptations as he rose in prominence. But his faithfulness in lesser responsibilities refined his integrity, preparing him for serving at the highest levels.

DEVELOPING THE CAPACITY TO HANDLE STRESS

Throughout his stressful experiences at Potiphar's house and later in prison, Joseph showed the kind of character that could make the best out of the worst situation.

God often uses times of stress to shape us. A number of years ago I spoke at a Labor Day weekend retreat for the United States Coast Guard Academy in Groton, Connecticut. There were a number of cadets there who had just come through their first "Swab Summer," the coast guard's version of boot camp. A swab is an entering freshman. These swabs had survived intense physical exercise and untold demands at the hands of upperclassmen. In one exercise they called "ZooLoo Drill," the swabs had to go through a series of quick uniform changes and inspections. One of the more unique exercises was called "Submarine Drill." When an upperclassman called out "Submarine Drill" at mealtime, all the swabs had to put their hands behind their backs and slurp their Jell-O. Now that really caught the attention of our children, who were with us on the retreat!

While sitting with the commander of the academy at lunch, I asked him the purpose of the Swab Summer. He said, "These cadets are headed for the most demanding, stressful, life-and-death situations that life can pose. Naturally, we can't create actual life-and-death situations, but we want to prepare the cadets by creating an environment in which they experience extreme pressure and learn how to respond with strength, clearheadedness, and creativity. They don't understand the purpose of what they're going through at the time. Later on, though, it all makes sense."

DEVELOPING THE CAPACITY TO LOOK FOR GOD'S WISDOM

In prison, in addition to having his own special dreams, Joseph learned to call upon the Lord to interpret dreams. When he learned that Pharaoh's cupbearer and baker, also in prison, were deeply troubled by their dreams, Joseph offered to interpret them, making it clear that he was doing so by the Spirit of God (see Genesis 40:8). Joseph had developed the capacity to look to God for wisdom.

You recall the story. Joseph said that the cupbearer's dream about a vine that grew three branches that bud-

ded, blossomed, and bore fruit meant that the cupbearer would be restored to Pharaoh's favor in three
days. On the other hand, the baker's dream of the birds
eating the baked goods from the basket on his head
meant that he would be killed in three days. And these
things happened just as Joseph said. Yet Joseph remained in prison, having been forgotten by the cupbearer.

Again, Joseph waited. But after two years, Pharaoh
himself had troubling dreams. Then the cupbearer re-
membered Joseph, who was brought before Pharaoh.
Joseph interpreted Pharaoh's dream as a warning of
coming famine. He also offered a plan to prepare for
the famine, a plan that brought him from the prison
cell to the highest place in Pharaoh's court.

Joseph seemed to have it made. Yet one more significant test, the hardest test of all, lay ahead for him.

DEVELOPING THE CAPACITY TO FORGIVE

A number of people had turned against Joseph over the
course of his life. He was abandoned by his brothers,
betrayed by Potiphar's wife, and rejected by Potiphar
himself. He was neglected by the cupbearer, who had
said he would remember Joseph for interpreting his
dream. Such experiences could obviously make a person bitter. But Joseph responded, not with bitterness,
but with forgiveness.

I am reminded of the powerful story of Corrie ten
Boom, the Dutch woman who, along with her sister
Betsie, was sent to a Nazi concentration camp for hiding
Jews in German-occupied Holland. In her classic book

The Hiding Place, ten Boom describes the events leading up to their incarceration—and the suffering she and Betsie underwent at the hands of the Nazi guards. She tells, for example, of the cruel treatment Betsie received when her failing health made it difficult for her to carry out the hard labor to which she had been assigned. One day, working on leveling some rough ground, a stumbling Betsie had struggled to lift even a tiny shovelful of dirt. A female guard screamed at her:

"Faster! . . . Loafer! Lazy swine!"

The guard snatched Betsie's shovel from her hands and ran from group to group of the digging crew, exhibiting the handful of dirt that was all Betsie had been able to lift.

"Look what Madame Baroness is carrying! Surely she will overexert herself!"

The other guards and even some of the prisoners laughed. Encouraged, the guard threw herself into a parody of Betsie's faltering walk. A male guard was with our detail today and in the presence of a man the women guards were always animated.

As the laughter grew, I felt a murderous anger rise. The guard was young and well fed—was it Betsie's fault that she was old and starving? But to my astonishment, Betsie too was laughing.

"That's me all right," she admitted, "But you'd better let me totter along with my little spoonful, or I'll have to stop altogether."

The guard's plump cheeks went crimson. "I'll

decide who's to stop!" And snatching the leather
crop from her belt she slashed Betsie across the
chest and neck.

Without knowing what I was doing I had seized
my shovel and rushed at her.

Betsie stepped in front of me before anyone
had seen. "Corrie!" she pleaded, dragging my
arm to my side. "Corrie, keep working!" She
tugged the shovel from my hand and dug it into
the mud. Contemptuously the guard tossed
Betsie's shovel toward us. I picked it up, still in a
daze. A red stain appeared on Betsie's collar; a
welt began to swell on her neck.

Betsie saw where I was looking and laid a bird-
thin hand over the whip mark. "Don't look at it,
Corrie. Look at Jesus only." She drew away her
hand: it was sticky with blood.[1]

Finally, Betsie's health broke. As she was placed on a
stretcher to be carried to the hospital, she said to Corrie,
"[We] must tell people what we have learned here. We
must tell them that there is no pit so deep that He is not
deeper still. They will listen to us, Corrie, because we
have been here."[2]

Betsie had developed the capacity to forgive. She
knew that bitterness is a poison of our own making. The
hurt we receive is one small ingredient. But mix in a
measure of pride, a dash of vengeance, a pinch of self-
pity, and an ounce of fear, and we have concocted a ma-
licious mixture that is certain to make us miserable.
There are those such as Corrie ten Boom's sister Betsie,

however, who discover the antidote. And when they do, they have a power that goes beyond anything this evil world can throw at them.

Joseph knew the antidote. When he eventually met his brothers again many years after they had sold him into slavery, instead of retaliating, he took them through a process of restoration. In one of the most memorable verses in the Bible, Joseph says to his brothers, "You intended to harm me, but God intended it for good to accomplish what is now being done, the saving of many lives" (Genesis 50:20, NIV). Joseph saw beyond his hurt to the hand of God.

WHERE WAS GOD IN ALL OF THIS?

God was developing capacities for leadership and wisdom in Joseph. He was also cultivating capacities for forgiveness, grace, reconciliation, and restoration—not only in Joseph's heart and for his family, but for the purposes of redemption! Saving a family and the world from famine pales in comparison to reconciling the covenant family and preserving the messianic line. What if Joseph had remained bitter? What if he had refused to feed his family? It could have spelled the end of Israel! God was in the whole process of Joseph's imprisonment, fulfilling God's own purpose of relieving not only a physical famine but a famine of the heart.

Looking back over this whole story, we stand in awe of God, who took a boastful nomad from a severely conflicted family and used him not only to save his people from famine but to prepare and perpetuate a holy nation.

What we too often fail to realize is that God wants more for us, far more than we could ever ask or imagine. And to give more to us, he must do more within us. W. E. Biederwolf reminds us that this is a common experience of God's people:

> If Jacob's desire had been given him in time for him to get a good night's sleep he might never have become the prince of prayers we know today. If Hannah's prayer for a son had been answered at the time she set for herself, the nation might never have known the mighty man of God it found in Samuel. Hannah wanted only a son, but God wanted more. He wanted a prophet, and a savior, and a ruler for His people. Someone said that "God had to get a woman before He could get a man." This woman He got in Hannah [by virtue of] those weeks and months and years [became] a woman with a vision like God's with tempered soul and gentle spirit and a seasoned will, prepared to be the kind of a mother for the kind of a man God knew the nation needed.[3]

IS THIS WHY MY PRAYER IS STILL UNANSWERED?

If you are expressing your heart's desire for things that are consistent with God's Word, you may well be in a season of preparation during which your answer is "ripening." More than likely, however, you will, like Jill in the story at the beginning of this chapter, be unable to discern just how you are being prepared while you are still waiting for an answer. But you can continue to pray in the confidence that God knows the best time.

The principle of preparation can be a great encouragement to faith. Let the story of Joseph sow seeds of expectation. By faith, imagine ways in which God might answer your prayers to bring great glory to himself and great joy to you.

HOW TO PRAY

How do you keep going in the meantime?

Look for God's encouragement in other places. For example, look at his answers to other prayers, including your "little" prayers. When I asked Jill what kept her going while she was waiting for an answer to her prayers, she shared how she saw "little" answers to her prayers about her job and her boys. "Those let me know God was still there and still working," she said.

Make the idea of preparation a matter for prayer. Pray words like these: "Lord, if there are things in me that need to change, I invite you to work in my heart, mind, soul, body, and circumstances." I have a friend who is now an author. She had published small articles for a number of years but never really got a break for publishing a book. She had a strong sense that the Lord would one day open that door. "In the meantime, I was to continue the work of preparation," she told me. "I was reading, writing, developing ideas, honing my skills, and developing my abilities of observation and expression."

Then, her first book was published, and many since then. That time of preparation lay the foundation that sustained her once the opportunities opened for her. "In fact," she says, "now I am so busy on projects that I have no time for additional preparation! I am so thankful I was as prepared as I was, or I think I may have had only one opportunity—and done poorly at it."

Listen to the Lord for leading about the subject of your prayer. Evaluate your prayer situation, both for perspective and insight. How desperate is this situation? How could God be glorified? Ask, "How does God want me to pray now?"

Invite others to carry the burden with you. Jill reached a point of desperation when she felt no choice but to reach out. Ideally, we are creating communities of faith, hope, and love where it is safe to share our needs, where prayer is offered and encouraged. We may feel it appropriate to choose just one person or a limited number of people for any particular prayer, but the message is clear: we are to bear one another's burdens.

Keep praying and intentionally seeking God's glory. This means surrendering our desires again on the altar of faith. When we put God's glory first, our anxiety lessens. We learn to acknowledge his prerogative in our life—and in the lives of others! He is Lord. He fully supports the revelation of his glory. So we pray earnestly, "Lord, bring your glory through this situation." This desire is the essence of the first petition in the Lord's

Prayer: "Hallowed be your name." We could para-phrase it as saying, "May the glory of your name come through all we seek."

Increase your faith. One suggestion for doing this is to paraphrase Martha's words to Jesus when she spoke to him following the death of Lazarus: "But even now I know that God will give you whatever you ask" (John 11:22). Say instead, "But even now I know that God will give [me] whatever [I] ask." This may seem presumptu-ous, but when affirmed in the spirit of humility, seeking God's glory, it is a means of building faith. As many have noted, faith is like a muscle: it needs exercise to grow. When we pray this way, we often become more sensitive to the content of our prayers as well.

Jesus' words to those standing near the risen Lazarus give us a wonderful picture of the power of anticipa-tion: "Unbind him, and let him go" (John 11:44, RSV). What a powerful image for answered prayer: Unwrap him from the death clothes—which made death seem like the final word, which were placed on him with tears of loss and despair. Set him free—free forever from the fear of death. Free from the doubt of God's love and power. Free to savor every moment of life.

On the other side of waiting is a life of confidence and joy with which nothing in this world compares! Imagine the changed outlook of Joseph and his brothers after they survived the famine in Egypt. They knew like no one else that the Lord works in mysterious ways to prepare his people for his purposes. They would join Jill and count-less others who say, "It's well worth the wait!"

NOTES

1. Corrie ten Boom (with John and Elizabeth Sherrill), *The Hiding Place* (Washington Depot, Conn.: Chosen Books, 1971), 185–86.

2. Ibid., 197.

3. W. E. Biederwolf, quoted in E. M. Bounds, *The Essentials of Prayer* (Grand Rapids: Baker Book House, 1979 reprint), 69.

CHAPTER SIX

The Principle of Selfishness

When I was about ten years old, I went to Sunday school one Sunday and heard the promise of Jesus, "Whatever you ask in my name, I will do it, that the Father may be glorified in the Son; if you ask anything in my name, I will do it" (John 14:13-14, RSV). "Whatever you ask . . ." Now THAT caught my attention. So I prayed and prayed. For what? A motorized go-cart and a color television set! How sad, you say. But to a fourth grader wrestling with prayer and the desires of his heart, this was no small matter. I couldn't understand why my prayers weren't answered. And as time went on, with no go-cart or color TV materializing, I wasn't sure what to make of prayer. The lack of answers to my prayers didn't send me into a crisis of faith, but it did make me ask one of the most common questions about prayer: *What if God doesn't want me to have what I want?*

The answer to this question is found in the book of James. "And even when you do ask, you don't get it because your whole motive is wrong—you want only what will give you pleasure" (James 4:3). In other words, God may say no to us because our requests are selfish.

Now this principle is not as simple as it seems. We can understand that selfishness blocks the answer to our prayers. But some people have the idea that it is always inappropriate to pray for themselves, that to do so would be selfish. In my experience, this is a widespread misperception. I've actually had to tell quite a few people that it's important for them to pray for themselves. So before we consider the problem of selfishness, let's look at the validity and necessity of prayer for ourselves.

IT'S NOT NECESSARILY SELFISH TO PRAY FOR YOURSELF

Praying for yourself is practical, important, and necessary for a number of reasons.

First, remember that God wants to care for you. James 4:2 says, "You do not have because you do not ask" (RSV). The implied message is that it is important for us to ask so that we can get what we need. This is the same message as Matthew 7:7, which promises us, "Ask, and it will be given you; seek, and you will find; knock, and it will be opened to you" (RSV).

What kinds of requests fall into the category of appropriate self-care rather than selfishness? According to Scripture, you can freely:

Pray for God to supply your material needs. "And this same God who takes care of me will supply all your needs from his glorious riches, which have been given to us in Christ Jesus" (Philippians 4:19.)

Pray for release from suffering and from Satan's attacks.

> So humble yourselves under the mighty power of God, and in his good time he will honor you. Give all your worries and cares to God, for he cares about what happens to you.
>
> Be careful! Watch out for attacks from the Devil, your great enemy. He prowls around like a roaring lion, looking for some victim to devour. Take a firm stand against him, and be strong in your faith. Remember that your Christian brothers and sisters all over the world are going through the same kind of suffering you are.
>
> In his kindness God called you to his eternal glory by means of Jesus Christ. After you have suffered a little while, he will restore, support, and strengthen you, and he will place you on a firm foundation. (1 Peter 5:6-10)

Pray for help with your problems. "Don't worry about anything; instead, pray about everything. Tell God what you need, and thank him for all he has done. If you do this, you will experience God's peace, which is far more wonderful than the human mind can understand. His peace will guard your hearts and minds as you live in Christ Jesus" (Philippians 4:6-7).

Pray for direction. "Trust in the Lord with all your heart; do not depend on your own understanding. Seek his will in all you do, and he will direct your paths" (Proverbs 3:5-6).

Pray for self-understanding and purification.
"Search me, O God, and know my heart; test me and
know my thoughts. Point out anything in me that of-
fends you, and lead me along the path of everlasting
life" (Psalm 139:23-24).

Pray for effective ministry. "And pray for me, too.
Ask God to give me the right words as I boldly explain
God's secret plan that the Good News is for the Gentiles,
too. I am in chains now for preaching this message as
God's ambassador. But pray that I will keep on speaking
boldly for him, as I should" (Ephesians 6:19-20).

Search the Bible, and you will find innumerable
promises encouraging you to come boldly before the
Lord with your needs and heart desires. It is not more
spiritual to overlook yourself, to play the martyr. Even
as loving parents delight in giving good gifts to their
children, so the Lord longs to care for you in practical
ways.

Second, when you trust God with your needs, you are
free to pursue his purposes. Matthew 6:33 assures us
that as we seek God's kingdom, God sees to our needs.
We are not expected to ignore our practical needs nor
to try to meet them apart from the Lord. A wise employer provides the tools and conditions necessary to
accomplish the job. College and professional athletes
are given the training facilities, instruction, equip-
ment, food, travel, and housing necessary to perform at
their peak. Part of God's plan is to set us free from
worldly concerns so that we will give ourselves fully to
his service. What does this mean for you? It may mean

that you will need to adjust your expectations, but it also means that God will supply your every need.

Third, God wants to supply your needs as a stimulus to worship, thanksgiving, and praise. We read in Psalm 50:15, "Call upon me in the day of trouble; I will deliver you, and you shall glorify me" (RSV). Our joy arises not only in response to God's answer but in *how* God answers our prayers. I think of the time our daughter, Kristen, applied for a job and went through three interviews. Naturally her expectations increased with every interview. So she was stunned when she got a call saying she wouldn't be hired. We prayed for her, and the next day her grandfather suggested she visit the employer and simply say, "I was very hopeful I would get this position and hope to get one like it in the future. Could you give me any feedback that would help me?" The next day Kristen went to see the employer, who greeted her very warmly. When she asked her question, he seemed very confused. Checking her file, he showed her that he had given the approval to hire her! Someone had called and given her mistaken information. But a similar position was open, and the employer hired Kristen for it immediately. God's answer stimulated Kristen's faith and praise to God.

I have seen God show his love in ways that amaze me, generating renewed gratitude and love for him. This is especially true in the answers to little prayers. I am convinced that love is revealed most clearly in the small things, the little touches that show we care. When a friend buys me a new book by one of my favorite authors, it shows that he has been thinking about me and paying attention to what I care about. God supplies our needs, even our small needs, as a testimony to his power and an evidence of his care.

Our family experienced God's care in a seemingly little thing when we visited Ireland one summer. My wife and I and our three boys had arrived in Dublin and needed to pick up a rental car across town for the rest of our trip. We faced a number of problems in trying to get the car. First, we weren't sure if all our luggage would fit into one car. We could rent a minivan, but it would cost literally three times as much. And we couldn't be sure which kind of vehicle we needed without having all our luggage at the rental garage. So how would we get the family and all our luggage there? If we took public transportation, we would have to walk a significant distance from our hotel and then make two bus transfers. That seemed like too much work. Sarah and I could take a taxi, but we wouldn't have all the luggage with us to determine if it would fit in the one car. We would also have to drive back across town to pick up the boys at the hotel. And taking two taxis would be quite expensive. Now, you may be better at logistics than I am, but as we considered our options, my head was spinning. We'd been traveling for a number of weeks, and I was weary. Sarah and I prayed with the boys at breakfast, asking God to figure it out for us. Then I went to the hotel desk and ordered a taxi. We'd just have to take it one step at a time. When the "taxi" arrived, it was a full-size van! I didn't even know such vehicles were available. We quickly loaded all our luggage into the van for the trip to the rental garage. The trip turned out to be much longer and more complicated than we had envisioned. It was such a relief to have all of us together. And, by the way, all our luggage did fit into the one car—with a few things on our laps! God was merciful to us weary travelers.

God enjoys showing his love in practical ways. When he does, our heart deepens in understanding and appreciation. He doesn't buy our love. He's already done that in Christ! But he does long to give us good things.

RECOGNIZING WHEN SELF IS GETTING IN THE WAY

How can we tell when a prayer is selfish? Here are some "markers":

Our prayer is selfish when the requested answer would benefit us at the expense of others. The classic example of this confronted me the first time I was asked to pray with a high school football team prior to a game. I knew that there were believers from our church youth group on both teams. How was I supposed to pray? Whose team was God on? It became obvious that to pray for the one team to win would be selfish. So instead, I led the team in a prayer focusing on sportsmanship, safety, and having a good time.

Of course there are times when our prayer concerns something we are seeking that others may want also, such as a job for which there are multiple applicants, or an apartment or house we want to live in. But an answer in our favor in many of these situations is not really at the expense of the other person. They may not get what they wanted, but it didn't take something from them they already had, nor something to which they had a greater right. Look more closely at praying for a particular job, for example: It would be selfish to pray for someone to fail so that you can take their place. It is not selfish, however, to pray for a position for which you believe yourself qualified, even if others are also applying.

Our prayer is selfish when our request presumes upon God's grace and goodness. James 4:13-16 speaks directly to the sin of taking daily life and the future for granted: "Look here, you people who say, 'Today or tomorrow we are going to a certain town and will stay there a year. We will do business there and make a profit.' How do you know what will happen tomorrow? For your life is like the morning fog—it's here a little while, then it's gone. What you ought to say is, 'If the Lord wants us to, we will live and do this or that.' Otherwise you will be boasting about your own plans, and all such boasting is evil."

God's desire is for us to focus on today and leave the future in his hands. The Lord's Prayer counsels us to pray for daily bread. We pray presumptuously when we "name and claim" a future blessing that somehow denies God's governance of our lives. I struggled through this concept with a friend who had been taught that if he would just name his desire and claim it by faith, it would be his. So he named a large business and began to claim it as his. He did some things that made him look very foolish and made his faith an object of ridicule by others. His dream never came to pass, and, sadly, he blames his lack of faith, rather than his misunderstanding of the nature of faith. Faith means turning to God in confidence that he will provide. It does not mean obligating God to fulfill our whims.

Our prayer is selfish when the request would benefit us in ways that are not consistent with God's values and direction for our life. There are some very unsettling answers to prayer in the Bible that reveal the danger of getting what we ask for. For example, when the Lord supplied manna to sustain the Israelites in the wilderness, they began to complain that they wanted meat. The Lord was angry with them but gave them what they wanted. We read what happened next in Numbers 11:31-34 :

> Now the Lord sent a wind that brought quail from the sea and let them fall into the camp and all around it! For many miles in every direction from the camp there were quail flying about three feet above the ground. So the people went out and caught quail all that day and throughout the night and all the next day, too. No one gathered less than fifty bushels! They spread the quail out all over the camp. But while they were still eating the meat, the anger of the Lord blazed against the people, and he caused a severe plague to break out among them. So that place was called Kibroth-hattaavah—"the graves of craving"—because they buried the people there who had craved meat from Egypt.

This is a troubling story. But we need to remember Paul's explanation of the story in 1 Corinthians 10:2-6 :

As followers of Moses, they were all baptized in the cloud and the sea. And all of them ate the same miraculous food, and all of them drank the same miraculous water. For they all drank from the miraculous rock that traveled with them, and that rock was Christ. Yet after all this, God was not pleased with most of them, and he destroyed them in the wilderness. These events happened as a warning to us, so that we would not crave evil things as they did.

The Israelites wanted a change of diet. They could have simply prayed, "Gracious God, you have provided for our need in every way. Your grace and supernatural power are shown us every morning. Lord, do not hear us as ungrateful, but we bring you our request that you provide meat for us. No matter what you do, Lord, we will be grateful." I don't think such a prayer would have been of line. To me, it was the Israelites' contentious tone and critical spirit, not their desire, that brought judgment upon them. The lesson for us is to listen for God's direction while we are praying.

UNLOCKING THE POWER OF SELFLESSNESS

Whereas many of the illustrations in this book are negative examples, we have a number of positive demonstrations of the power of selflessness. In Acts 4:31-35, for example, we see how selflessness in the early church unleashed great power in the community of faith:

After this prayer, the building where they were meeting shook, and they were all filled with the Holy Spirit. And they preached God's message with boldness.

All the believers were of one heart and mind, and they felt that what they owned was not their own; they shared everything they had. And the apostles gave powerful witness to the resurrection of the Lord Jesus, and God's great favor was upon them all. There was no poverty among them, because people who owned land or houses sold them and brought the money to the apostles to give to others in need.

Selflessness empties our hands so the Lord can fill them. It also helps us develop a level of love, trust, and support in the community that fuels incredible power in prayer.

One of my favorite stories about boldness empowered by selflessness is that of Martin Luther's prayer for his good friend, Frederick Myconius. In 1540, Myconius became deathly sick. One night, expecting that he would die within a short time, Myconius wrote, with trembling hand, a fond farewell to Luther, whom he loved very much.

When Luther received the letter, he immediately sent back the following reply: "I command thee in the name of God to live because I still have need of thee in the work of reforming the church. . . . The Lord will never let me hear that thou art dead, but will permit thee to survive me. For this I am praying, this is my will, and may my will be done, because I seek only to glorify the name of God."

Myconius had already lost the faculty of speech when Luther's letter came. But in a short time he was well again. And in keeping with his friend's prayer, he survived Luther by two months![1]

Nothing makes us so bold in prayer as when we can look into the eye of God and say to him, "Thou knowest that I am not praying for personal advantage, nor to avoid hardship, nor that my own will in any way should be done, but only for this, that Thy name might be glorified."[2]

When we seek the glory of the Lord, we discover a freedom and boldness we may have never thought possible.

IS THIS WHY MY PRAYER IS STILL UNANSWERED?

As you consider a specific request, search your heart. Test your motives with the questions from this chapter:

- Would this request benefit me at the expense of others?
- Does this request presume upon God's grace and goodness?
- Would this request benefit me in ways that do not match God's values and direction for my life?

I was speaking with a Christian consultant who felt he was finally doing what he wanted to do, combining his vocational skills and his love of travel by consulting with Christian workers around the country and sometimes overseas. He had come to see me about some struggles he was having with one of the organizations he was serving. He had some tough personnel decisions to recommend but found himself unwilling to make them. It wasn't clear why when we first started talking, but in the course of conversation it became clear that his recommendations could cost him his lucrative consulting contract. "I realize I have not been open to doing whatever needs to be done because I really want to keep this position," he said. "That's why I haven't known how to pray."

As we talked the situation through, this man came to see several things. First, he saw that God had entrusted his position to him in the first place. Therefore, he had to do the right thing to honor the Lord. Second, he saw that he had begun to hold the things he enjoyed too tightly, allowing them to take the place of full reliance and availability to God.

As you pray about situations in your own life, ask yourself: *How would I expect to benefit from this prayer? How could my desired answer to this prayer affect others? What would that answer do to me? What would it do to my relationship with God, my family, and those with whom I am trying to share Christ?*

HOW THEN DO I PRAY?

Here are some suggestions for praying unselfishly:

Hold your requests loosely. One of the most important means to personal peace is yielding to the Lord. This is not easy, but it is essential. When we care more about our requests than about our relationship with the Lord, we have crossed the line of selfishness. We are trying to use God to get what we want. But when we present our requests in confidence and humility, we find the peace that surpasses understanding. When we hold our requests loosely, prayer is more like a conversation with a loving parent than a transaction with a commercial retailer. That does not mean that we don't care about the outcome. It just means that we care more about maintaining our relationship with the Lord than about getting our own way, that we are open to the Lord's revealing of a better way to pray or providing a different solution.

Ask in Jesus' name. Remember the promise that got me praying for a go-cart and a color TV? "Whatever you ask in my name, I will do it, that the Father may be glorified in the Son; if you ask anything in my name, I will do it" (John 14:13-14, RSV). I was emphasizing the "whatever you ask" phrase when I should have been emphasizing the "in my name" phrase. What does it mean to ask in Jesus' name? It means praying as if Jesus were making the request. Consider: what would Jesus ask for? What would he be concerned about? How would he pray for this situation?

Consider the welfare of others. As a husband and father, I know that my prayers must continually take into account my family. As a pastor, I know my prayers must continually keep in mind the people whom I serve. When I forget others, my prayers go off track.

While selfishness chokes the air supply of prayer, selflessness breathes new life into our petitions and intercessions. To paraphrase a famous exhortation, do not ask what God can do for you, but ask what God wants you to do for his glory and for others. In dying to self-ishness, we come alive to the joy of being partners with God. In the process, our heart finds a satisfaction and a peace that nothing else can supply.

NOTES

1. O. Hallesby, *Prayer* (Minneapolis: Augsburg Publishing House, 1931), 130–31.

2. Ibid.

CHAPTER SEVEN

Living with Unanswered Prayer

There is a risk in analyzing prayer as we have done in this book, a risk that we will spend more time trying to understand prayer than we will praying. And as we focus on the reasons behind unanswered prayer, it would be easy to forget that God answers prayer! That's why it's so important to draw inspiration from the accounts of God's marvelous answers to the petitions of his people. One such account was given by a medical missionary who told the following story while back on furlough, visiting his home church in Michigan:

> While serving at a small field hospital in Africa, every two weeks I traveled by bicycle though the jungle to a nearby city for supplies. This was a journey of two days, which required camping overnight at the halfway point.
>
> On one of these journeys I arrived in the city where I planned to collect money from a bank, purchase medicine and supplies, and then begin

my two-day journey back to the field hospital.
Upon arrival in the city, I observed two men
fighting, one of whom had been seriously
injured. I treated him for his injuries, and at the
same time witnessed to him of the Lord Jesus
Christ. I then traveled two days, camping
overnight, and arrived home without incident.

Two weeks later I repeated my journey. Upon
arriving in the city, I was approached by the
young man I had treated two weeks earlier. He
told me that he had known that I carried money
and medicines. He said, "Some friends and I
followed you into the jungle, knowing that you
would camp overnight. We were waiting just
outside your campsite for you to go to sleep. We
planned to kill you and take your money and
drugs. But just as we were about to move into
your campsite, we saw that you were surrounded
by twenty-six armed guards."

At this, I laughed and said that I was certainly
all alone out in the jungle campsite. The young
man pressed the point, however, and said, "No
sir, I was not the only person to see the guards.
My five friends also saw them, and we all counted
them. It was because of those guards that we were
afraid and left you alone. . . ."

At this point in the church presentation in
Michigan, one of the men in the church jumped
to his feet and interrupted the speaker. He asked,
"Sir, can you tell me the exact day that this
incident happened?" It took the missionary a

moment to recall, but he could. When he informed the congregation of the date, the man who had interrupted him told this story:

"When it is night in Africa, it is day here. On the night of your incident in Africa, it was morning here and I was preparing to go play a game of golf. As I was putting my golf bag in the car, I felt the Lord leading me to pray for you. In fact, the urging of the Lord was so strong, I called the men in this church together to meet with me here in the sanctuary and pray for you. Would all of those men who met with me on that day please stand up?"

The men who met together to pray that day stood. When all were counted, the number was twenty-six!

"Are they not all ministering spirits, sent out to render service for the sake of those who will inherit salvation?" (Hebrews 1:14, NASB).[1]

God answers prayer! And even when he doesn't answer prayer for a time, he is still engaging us in vital fellowship and spiritual growth. So we have good reason to pray quickly, confidently, and boldly. I am stirred by the words of E. M. Bounds:

> Great faith enables Christ to do great things. We need a quickening of faith in God's power. We have hedged God in till we have little faith in His power. We have conditioned the exercise of His power till we have a little God, and a little faith in a little God.

The only condition which restrains God's power, and which disables Him to act, is unfaith.

In God's ability to do, He goes far beyond men's ability to ask. No commonplace tameness should restrain our largest asking. Large, larger, and largest asking magnifies grace and adds to God's glory. Feeble asking impoverishes the asker, and restrains God's purposes for the greatest good, and obscures His glory.[2]

EXERCISING GREAT FAITH IN THE FACE OF UNANSWERED PRAYER

I realize that I haven't addressed all the reasons for unanswered prayer in this book. I may not have touched on the reason that affects your situation. But as we look at how to live with unanswered prayer—whatever the reason for it—I hope that you are encouraged both to search your own soul and to spend time with the Lord and the Bible seeking insight.

To get insight into living with unanswered prayer, let's look at Paul's response to an unanswered prayer in 2 Corinthians 12:7-10. Paul relates his experience of being caught up into the third heaven. But then he faced a time of trial and unanswered prayer. He writes:

> But to keep me from getting puffed up, I was given a thorn in my flesh, a messenger from Satan to torment me and keep me from getting proud.
>
> Three different times I begged the Lord to take it away. Each time he said, "My gracious

favor is all you need. My power works best in your weakness." So now I am glad to boast about my weaknesses, so that the power of Christ may work through me. Since I know it is all for Christ's good, I am quite content with my weaknesses and with insults, hardships, persecutions, and calamities. For when I am weak, then I am strong.

Three principles emerge from Paul's story that may help you live with unanswered prayer.

MAKE PRAYER YOUR FIRST RESPONSE

Paul did not accept his "thorn" like a Stoic. He begged God to take it from him. We should never hesitate to bring our requests immediately to the Lord.

As you are living with unanswered prayer, keep praying. Don't hesitate to pray about anything and everything. Some people say, "Well, why should I pray when God already knows what I need?" The answer is, because God likes to be asked. P. T. Forsyth notes, "Love loves to be told what it knows already. . . . It wants to be asked for what it longs to give."[3]

Why would a parent who knows his or her child needs something delay giving it until the child asks? There are many good reasons. The delay can teach the child initiative and how to take responsibility for his own life. It may be a way to engage the child in conversation about the nature of the request and other possible ways to meet his need. Jesus demonstrated this principle when he asked the blind beggar, "What do you want me to do for you?" (Mark 10:51). The blind man's need seemed so obvious, yet Jesus wanted more than "a satisfied customer"—he wanted to connect with the man in need. Frank Laubach, an early-twentieth-century missionary who developed methods of literacy education that are still used today, captures this desire in the following meditation:

> As I lay on the warm earth on Signal Hill last night I asked God the question:
>
> "Why is it that Thou dost allow us on this earth to do nearly all the talking? Why do we not always hear Thy voice, since Thou art so much wiser than we are?"
>
> Instantly back came the answer. I could see it, from beginning to end, in a second, though it may require more than a minute to write it down. So many of these thoughts from God are hurled at me in an instant like that:
>
> "When you are teaching the Moros to read, your art is to say as little as you can and leave them to say as much as they will. That is why I leave you to do and say as much as you can, while I say little. You learn by doing, even when you make mistakes and correct them. You are to be sons and daughters of God, and now you are taking the first feeble steps of infants. Every step you take alone is infinitely more important than you now imagine, because the thing I am preparing you for exceeds all your imagination.

So the talking you do to me is essential. The talking others do to you, when they are trying to talk up to your expectations, is more important than the talks you give to them. This is the best way to act: Talk a great deal to me. Let others talk a great deal to you, appreciating everything fine they say and neglecting their mistakes."[4]

God wants our talk. He wants prayer. He wants to hear our requests. It's the relationship, not simply the fulfillment of a request, that matters most. Love loves to be told what it already knows. I still ask my wife, Sarah, "Do you really love me?" And she will say, "You know I love you." Love wants to be asked for what it longs to give.

DON'T DEVALUE YOUR REQUESTS

One of our natural tendencies is to try to gauge how important our need really is to the Lord. Is it really worthy of his attention? Is it too small to bother him with? Paul's experience sheds light on this. He urges us to bring every concern to the Lord.

We do not know for certain the exact nature of Paul's malady, his "thorn in the flesh," and I think that's good. I believe the Scriptures are deliberately vague. Knowing human nature leads me to believe that if we knew what Paul was struggling with, we would either pass judgment on Paul or on God for not answering Paul's prayer. We aren't told because such things aren't for us to know and judge. Instead, we are presented with the testimony of a person dealing with an unspecified problem that was very difficult for him.

No one but you truly knows how difficult your problems are for you. And you don't know how difficult my problems are for me. We need to show each other grace in terms of our different responses to difficulties. Some of us have high thresholds for pain and frustration, while others of us have low thresholds. It is not for us to judge one another's thresholds. Think of the plant world: some plants are hearty and can live almost anywhere. Others, such as orchids, require extremely delicate handling. They are sensitive to the least change in climate, water, and soil conditions. So it is with individuals and with their requests. Some are more hearty than others in certain areas. We are not to judge one another in these matters. We are to support and encourage one another. Above all, we can be thankful that God cares about the least thing that troubles us. Above all, we can be assured that God respects our requests.

PRAY CONTINUALLY

Paul said, "I prayed three times." Some have taken this passage to mean that there is a limit to the number of times we can pray for something. Some have even said we can pray only three times. This is an inappropriate conclusion. Paul prayed until he heard God's answer. Then he stopped. It happened that he prayed three times before getting an answer, but we might pray thirty, three hundred, or even three thousand times until God impresses his response on our heart. My friend Pastor Paul Binnion gave me a phrase to encourage continual prayer: PUSH. *Pray Until Something Happens.* I like that. Effective prayer isn't a matter of quantity. It's a matter of continuing communication with the living Lord.

LISTEN FOR GOD'S RESPONSE

Each time Paul prayed, God's response was: "My gracious favor is all you need. My power works best in your weakness" (2 Corinthians 12:9). Paul's main need was God's sustaining power, not release from the problem. That same principle applies to us in many circumstances. We may not understand it, we may not like it, but we need to learn to live with it. Sometimes our problems are our lifeline to God.

I was meeting with a group of men when one asked, "What keeps your attention on the Lord?" Without hesitation, another man spoke up, "Being broken! When I'm struggling, God gets my full attention." We all identified with his confession. In our brokenness, we often discover God in ways we never would otherwise.

Do you ever wrestle with a sense of God's silence or withdrawal? What you are experiencing is a spiritual dynamic but not a theological reality. In other words, just because something may be part of your experience doesn't mean it's true. While you may feel that God is absent, the Scripture says in no uncertain terms that God never leaves you. You say, "How can you say that, Doug?" Well, let's look at Hebrews 13:5 (NIV), "Never will I leave you; never will I forsake you." Then there's Matthew 28:20: "I am with you always." If you sense God's silence, remember to rely on the truth of Scripture, not on your feelings.

TRUST GOD TO WORK THROUGH THE PROBLEM

Although he didn't remove Paul's problem, God promised to reveal his power through it. Paul discovered God's grace in ways he never could have apart from his unanswered prayer.

As in Paul's situation, unanswered prayer is often an occasion for grace. I was talking with a couple I'll call Scott and Sarah, who had been very successful in real estate until the market began a decline. After years of scrambling, they lost everything and had to file for bankruptcy. "We prayed and prayed and prayed," Scott said to me, "but God never answered our prayers the way we thought he should. Still, we learned more about his love and sustaining grace through that time than we ever had before." Scott and Sarah genuinely celebrated God's sustaining power, carrying them through the darkest days of their lives—even when they lost their house. God led them to a nice home they could afford, and they set up housekeeping on a greatly reduced basis—without a shred of resentment. Scott became bolder and bolder, both in sharing his struggle and in challenging others to seek the support they need in crisis. "Through this process, we realized that the family of God doesn't like to talk about failure, especially financial failure," Scott explained. "We're ready to help people be honest and get the help they need." Like Paul, Scott and Sarah found that our weakness may be God's greatest asset.

Let me make a very bold statement. I believe there is no such thing as unanswered prayer when we want what

God wants. We may have to wait, or we may have to revise our requests, or we may have to humble ourselves in the face of great mysteries, or we may have to repent, or we may have to go through a process of shaping and growth. But no matter what, we are to be in vital relationship with God, seeking his face and trusting his grace in all things.

The challenge is getting to that point.

I want to offer you the opportunity to come once again to God. I invite you to try a "holy experiment" in prayer, using a concept from a story I once heard about the beloved Episcopal teacher-preacher Dr. Sam Shoemaker, who was a primary developer of the Twelve Steps of Alcoholics Anonymous. One day Sam was talking with a man at his wits' end, who only kept going through a steady diet of pills and liquor. He saw no way out of his predicament. The man knew Shoemaker was a Christian, so when Sam asked, "Want to try an experiment?" he waved him off, saying, "Oh, I don't believe in God."

Sam said, "Well, there is something that seems to help people, and that something will help you if you will let him."

"How can I let him if I don't believe in him?" asked the man.

"Well," said Sam, "suppose we try saying out loud the whole truth about your situation, the way you feel about it, to whatever the ultimate reality is in this universe. Call it 'he,' 'she,' or 'it' for the moment and honestly ask for help and guidance."

"Now how would you do that?" asked the skeptic as he grew a little warmer to the idea. Shoemaker suggested they kneel as an expression of reverence toward the unknown and then asked the man to say exactly what he was thinking and feeling, not putting on anything or pretending to believe something he did not believe. He was just to address himself to whatever creative force runs through the universe.

"Well, I certainly am in a jam," said the man. "I'll try anything once." Half laughing to himself, the man then knelt down, thinking nothing would happen but hoping with all his heart that it might. And there he prayed this prayer:

"Oh God, if there is a God, send me help now because I need it." In commenting upon that prayer, Shoemaker said, "It was a good, honest, selfish prayer. But from where I sit it is worth a dozen pious word formulations that never get above the ceiling."

Climbing back into his chair, the man looked at Shoemaker in a mischievous sort of a way and said, "I don't feel any different." Sam answered that he didn't especially care how he felt, but he was interested in what he was going to do. The man asked, "Got a Bible I can read?"

Later that former skeptic moved on to become a knowledgeable, contagious Christian. But it all began when he dared to be honest with God about his doubt, brought his deepest need to God, and opened his heart just a crack so as to allow God to plant his seeds of faith in his needy life. It was this man's way of saying, "Lord, I believe. Help me with my unbelief."

If you have given up praying about something, I want to encourage you to give it another try. Even if you are very disappointed in God, I urge you to come back to him, to let him touch you, as he did Paul, to let his power be shown in your weakness.

What situation troubles you? Bring it again to the Lord. Only this time, lay it gently on the altar of his grace. Let him search your heart. Listen for any prompts from the Holy Spirit about how you might change your prayer. Consider journaling your thoughts as a way to focus your prayer.

I leave you with a testimony from Diane. While she and her son Brian were driving home from a holiday visit with family members, something happened—she still isn't sure what—as they rounded a curve in the country road. The car went up an embankment and flipped over, breaking Diane's neck and killing Brian. Words cannot express Diane's anguish or the pain of other family members. But God sustained her, and she recovered. After preaching on unanswered prayer I received a note from Diane that greatly encouraged me. She wrote:

> Through months of grief and confinement,
> God repeatedly said, "Be still and know that
> I am God," and "God will give us His peace
> that surpasses all understanding." I was not
> to question God. I was to trust Him.
>
> God sent me special reassurance three months
> later in pictures Brian had taken himself. One
> was of Brian's hand with a "thumbs up" and
> another of a ceramic angel blowing a kiss. Brian

was OK and he's definitely with God. What more could a mother ask for?

Satan still tries to defeat me with whys and guilt, but God is stronger. . . . The truth is that we won't know the answers until we are in heaven. We must just trust God in all the good and bad and continue to seek him and study his Word.

What a powerful testimony of acceptance and courage. Diane learned that unanswered prayer isn't the last word. The Lord himself is our answer, our yes in all circumstances. Trust in the Lord, and you will break the bonds of discouragement, of unbelief, of withdrawal from God. And, wonder of wonder, God will use unanswered prayer to answer your deepest prayer to become more like Christ, growing ever stronger on the way.

NOTES

1. Reported by the Calvary Missionary Service in the "Global Prayer Digest," September 1991, U.S. Center of World Mission.

2. E. M. Bounds, *The Possibilities of Prayer* (Grand Rapids: Baker Book House, 1979 reprint), 61, 63, 66.

3. P. T. Forsyth, *The Soul of Prayer* (Grand Rapids: William B. Eerdmans Publishing Company, 1916), 63.

4. Frank C. Laubach, Ph. D., *Letters by a Modern Mystic* (New York: Student Volunteer Movement, 1937), 40.

ABOUT THE AUTHOR

Dr. Douglas J. Rumford is senior pastor of the innovative Colonial Presbyterian Church in Kansas City, Missouri, which has a congregation worshiping and growing at two sites. He has pastored for over 22 years, serving congregations in Fresno, California; Old Greenwich, Connecticut; and Faifield, Connecticut. He also served for a brief time as acquisitions director for nonfiction books at Tyndale House Publishers. Doug speaks frequently at conferences and conducts a variety of seminars.

Doug is the author of several books, including *SoulShaping* and *Questions God Asks, Questions Satan Asks,* both published by Tyndale House. Doug has also written a number of articles for such publications as *New Man* magazine, *Moody* magazine, *Christianity Today,* and *Leadership* journal.

Doug received his doctor of ministry degree from Fuller Theological Seminary. He earned his master of divinity degree from Gordon-Conwell Theological Seminary, graduating *summa cum laude* as valedictorian of his class, and a bachelor of arts degree from Miami University, Oxford, Ohio.

Doug and his wife, Sarah, have been married twenty-five years and have four children. Doug's goal in ministry is to touch hearts and minds with the truth, grace, and power of God: "As I serve Jesus Christ, my greatest joy is bringing ideas to life that can change lives."

Books by Douglas J. Rumford
and
Tyndale House Publishers

Questions God Asks, Questions Satan Asks

SoulShaping

What about Heaven and Hell?

What about Spiritual Warfare?

What about Unanswered Prayer?

What I Want You to Know